C000174989

THE RIDDLE OF SPHINX ROCK

The life and times of Great Gable

Ronald Turnbull

THE RIDDLE OF SPHINX ROCK
The life and times of Great Gable

with drawings by Colin Brash

Millrace

First published in Great Britain in 2005 by
Millrace
2a Leafield Road, Disley
Cheshire SK12 2JF
www.millracebooks.co.uk

ISBN: 1 902173 19 8

Typeset in Adobe Garamond Pro.
Printed and bound in the United Kingdom
by Cromwell Press Ltd, Trowbridge, Wiltshire.

Acknowledgements

Thanks to my father for first taking me up there, to Matt Scase and Barbara Turnbull for revising my route up Napes Needle and taking pictures, and to Colin Brash for going first on the awkward step into Arrowhead Gully, for his attractive illustrations, and for the unpleasant experience at the end of Chapter 6. Thanks, as always, to the National Trust and Lake District National Park Authority rangers and path teams.

Chapter 1 has appeared, in a slightly different form, in *TGO* (The Great Outdoors) magazine. Thanks to Frances Lincoln Ltd for allowing me to quote from the master, A Wainwright, on pages 10, 16, 164 and 165; to Joss Naylor (page 49), Alain de Botton (page 119) and Colin Mortlock (pages 171–2) for lines from their works; and to Sandra Griffin-Parr, daughter of A Harry Griffin, for the quotations from the other master on page 141.

RT

Advice to readers

Fellwalking, fellrunning and, especially, scrambling, are not completely safe; judging the risks against the likely pleasures is part of the point of it. Walkers and scramblers should satisfy themselves that they have the necessary skills and equipment: instruction in this is not part of the aim of this book. Despite Haskett Smith and the picture in Chapter 14, the Napes Needle is a serious climb that would normally be undertaken with ropes and belays.

The sketch maps are based on an out-of-copyright Bartholomew's half-inch sheet, and are not intended for navigation on the hill.

Paths and stiles can change. I'll be happy to hear of any updates or corrections, through the publishers.

RT

Contents

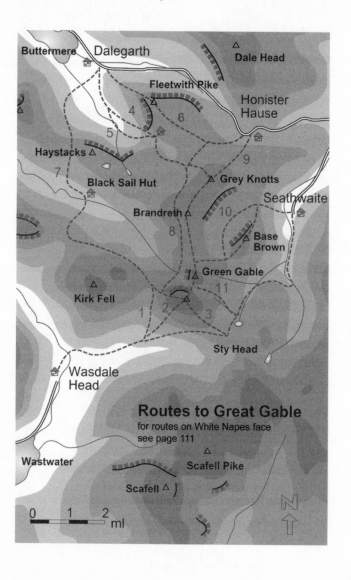

Buttermere Dalegarth
Dale Head

Fleetwith Pike

Honister Hause

4
6

5

Haystacks

9

7
Black Sail Hut
Grey Knotts

Seathwaite

Brandreth
10

8
Base Brown

Green Gable

11

Kirk Fell

1 2 3

Sty Head

Wasdale Head

Routes to Great Gable
for routes on White Napes face
see page 111

Wastwater
Scafell Pike

Scafell

0   1   2
ml

N

Introduction

The greatness of Gable

'Grand to look at, grand to look from, and grand to climb'—so Gable was described over a hundred years ago. It's the hill that has been the birthplace of two separate sorts of hill sport, and that today receives some 20,000 ascents each year.

This book is an exploration of Great Gable: its eleven main ways for walkers, its scrambles and its climbs.

But it's also a study of what it means to be a mountain in today's world. Cultural biographies are already on my shelves for Snowdon, Everest and Ben Nevis. Each of these is its country's high point. But in England, rather than Scafell Pike, I've preferred to walk up into the life and times of Great Gable. Here is England's finest viewpoint, and its iconic pinnacle. Its two faces, the Great Napes and Gable Crag, express the light and the dark of rock climbing. Many fine hills have fine ales named for them: but Great Gable isn't just a beer, it's a brewery. For many, myself included, Gable was the first hill; for many, too, Gable is the last resting place of our ashes.

I find I recognise mountains more easily than human beings; and maybe Great Gable is occupying a slot in my brain designed for an acquaintance of my own species. But Gable is a place, not a person. Accordingly, out of the many ways I could have described it (historically, or geologically, or even alphabetically) I have chosen clockwise. Ascents are described out of Wasdale, then round via Buttermere and Honister to Borrowdale, before homing in on the Great Napes.

Arbitrarily, I've included Green Gable, Brandreth, Grey Knotts and even Fleetwith Pike as foothills of Great Gable. Each of these can reasonably be crossed on a walk whose real aim is Gable. And it would be a shame to miss out Fanny Mercer's interesting alpenstock accident.

Life, death, and fellwalking: the great questions all ask themselves on Great Gable. And first among those questions is the Riddle of Sphinx Rock: what did we come up here for anyhow?

Sphinx Rock from the Screes Path

ROUTE 1 via Beck Head from Wasdale

Start: Wasdale Head
Distance to summit: 4km (2½ miles)
Total ascent: 820m (2,700ft)
Terrain: Steep stony paths, scree and boulder.

How good? This route avoids all Gable's most interesting aspects for a relentless plod to the summit.

From Wasdale Head, head upstream to the right of Lingmell Beck, forking right after 200 metres on a smaller path to pass left of Burnthwaite Farm. After 1½km comes a long footbridge over Gable Beck. Straight after this, turn left, up through a gate, to climb the steep south-west spur of Gable. At the 450m contour, the path turns left, to slant up the valley side of the Gable Beck and reach Beck Head col. The tarns at Beck Head are often dry, but there is a spring just to the right of where the path reaches the col.

From the right-hand end of the Beck Head col, a wide scree path slants up left to the steep north-west spur of Gable. It joins the spur at a grassy platform with a single iron fencepost, with the Moses Trod path descending beyond. But for the summit, head right, straight up the steep spur, on eroded paths. The way is on stones and scree, then through large boulders to the summit plateau.

Great Gable from Pillar

1 The Riddle of Sphinx Rock

'What goes on four legs in the morning, on two at noon, and in the evening on two legs and two walking poles?' Given 2,000 years to think about it, the original Riddle of the Sphinx is not really all that tricky. The Riddle of Sphinx Rock is tougher, though. And it's posed to anyone on any of the surrounding slopes. 'Just how great is Gable?' Or, to put it another way, 'What on earth are you up here for?'

Answers are important, even if they always come afterwards and contradict each other. With the invention of Alpinism, climbers could stop carrying aneroids and measuring the boiling point of water all the way up. With the discovery of Picturesque Beauty, early Lakes tourists no longer needed to make notes on the blacklead mine holes and the quaint customs of the Cumbrians. Today, the aim of it all is, apparently, to stand among the orange peel alongside some summit cairn.

Are we going up Gable to tick it off our list? No, because we've been up Gable several times already. Are we going up it for the view? If that were the case, then it'd be Westmorland Cairn that had the trample marks and the occasional abandoned boot, rather than the summit knoll.

Wainwright had a thing about Haystacks, but overall Gable must be Lakeland's most-loved mountain. Whatever it is we go up hills for, it's something that Great Gable has and that Great End, by comparison, lacks.

For starters, there's the shape. From Wasdale, it's the original and architectural gable end—from everywhere else, it's a sort of bowler hat—but always recognisable, and always important and big. We like the look of certain of our fellow humans: I might mention Johnny Depp, I might mention Meg Ryan. Depending on your gender preference, Johnny and Meg appeal to certain obvious and explainable instincts. Great Gable appeals to an instinct that, for now, remains nameless. It's like the Matterhorn, and Snowdon and the Cobbler, in having a shape that makes you want to get your leg up over it.

Skiddaw too is shapely: but Skiddaw is spoilt by having an easy way up. Gable plays a better game. Every path (except the rebuilt Breast Path from Sty Head) has boulders, scree and bare rock. Every path (and now including the Breast Path) involves steep ground. As the bowler-hat outline indicates, that steepness is at the top; and so every path involves an eagle's eye view back across the valley and the lake.

Almost irrelevant in all this is Great Gable's rocky little top knoll, the clear pool it once harboured now trampled by 20,000 pairs of Brashers. That so-sought summit stands a just-not-made-it 899m high, in its desert of stones, with its view of the inside of a cloud. Even if the cloud temporarily rises, all it reveals is an awful lot of stones, quite a few cairns, the edges of the plateau, and some similar stones on top of Scafell Pike.

'What are you up to?' asks the Sphinx. We thought we wanted to get to the top. Gable shows us that the answer's more complicated than that. Indeed, for the very greatest of Gable, the trick is to avoid ever having to arrive at all. Skirt Gable on the Screes Path, high above Wasdale with that wonderful Wasdale view, rock overhead, rock underfoot, and you don't even have to go uphill much. On the Ennerdale side there's the Climbers' Traverse, right up under the crags and getting dripped on by the overhangs.

Then consider all the other great places on Gable that aren't its top. Seek out the cave with the spring, halfway up the southern screes. Seek out the Hanging

Stone, and Moses Finger, and Moses' one-time hut somewhere on Gable Crag. Go into little Gillercomb, suspended halfway up the side of Borrowdale. Crouch behind a boulder in Windy Gap, from where steep paths drop east and west, other steep paths climb north and south.

We go to the tops of the hills for the sake of the going, not for the tops. The greatness of Gable is in the places along the way. The answer to the difficult question is nothing to do with the cairn on top—Gable often doesn't even have a cairn. But it is something to do with Westmorland Cairn, Sour Milk Gill and the Napes Needle. To solve the riddle, simply consider the Sphinx Rock.

ROUTE 2 Gavel Neese White Napes

Start:	Wasdale Head
Distance to summit:	3km (2 miles)
Total ascent:	820m (2,700ft)
Terrain:	Steep stony paths, scree and rock: with optional Grade 1 scrambling.

How good? Arduous, but interesting.

For the mountain scrambler pure and simple the White Napes provides a fascinating way up the Gable.
George Abraham, *British Mountain Climbs,* 1909

White Napes…has no notable crags and little of interest.
A Wainwright, *The Western Fells,* 1966

From Wasdale Head, head upstream to the right of Lingmell Beck, forking right after 200 metres on a smaller path. After 1½km comes a long footbridge over Gable Beck. Straight after this, turn off left to climb the steep south-west spur of Gable. At the 450m contour you reach the contouring Screes Path (Route 12).

The comfortable way now is to take the Screes Path to the left, contouring across screes to reach Beck Head. The uncomfortable way is to take the Screes Path to the right, to reach Little Hell Gate (Route 15). However, the direct and adventurous will head up the grass and broken rocks of the White Napes. The spur rises to a final tower. For a scramble, Grade 1, this can be attacked on its left flank for 15m, when an exposed ledge leads across right to easier ground. More easily, contour left around the foot of the tower to go up a short scree behind it.

The top of the tower is a grassy ridge with perched boulders. Go up the ridge to the main mountain, where a scree path leads up immediately left of Westmorland Crag—or the rocks to the right of the path can be scrambled. Contour right, along the crag top, to reach Westmorland Cairn, and head uphill to the summit.

2 Pinnacles of perfection

Plato was no fellwalker. His sport of choice is indicated by his Metaphor of the Cave. In *The Republic*, he describes how he sat in some Greek equivalent of Gaping Gill, watching the flickering shadows made by fellow potholers, all of whom had burnt out their helmet torches except for the chap at the back. What we see are shadows: the real world is behind us and unknowable.

What is dog? We can look at an entity of the real world and say, 'Yes, that is an example of dog,' or 'No, that one is human being.' More, we can say, 'Yes, that is dog, but with fewer legs, more hair, even noisier.' This is possible because there is, in the realm of pure thought, an Idea of Dog. Only the Idea is completely real. Unfortunately, it is also completely unknowable. Any specific dog is dog insofar as it corresponds with the Idea of Dog. Thus the Ideal Dog has exactly four legs, is somewhere between hairy and fluffy, barks but not all the time, and so on.

And the Ideal Mountain is shaped like the Matterhorn.

Mountains that approach the ideal are nicknamed accordingly. Grisedale Pike is the 'Lakeland Matterhorn'; Belles Knott is the 'Matterhorn of Langdale'. Elsewhere, Sgurr na Ciche is the Knoydart Matterhorn, Cnicht is the Welsh Matterhorn, Yarigatake is the Matterhorn of Japan.

Great Gable, also, approaches this ideal of mountain form, a straight-sided triangle, breaking into crag for the upper third. At least, it does so when seen from Wasdale alongside its shapely sidekick Yewbarrow. (The Matterhorn itself is only the Matterhorn when seen from Zermatt: from anywhere else it has noticeable flat bits on the way up.) Gable pretends to be a classic pointy peak—thus living up to its name. For in the original Norse, Gavel was not only the fairly pointy end wall of your house, but also the very pointy bows of your boat.

But when it comes to the Platonically perfect pinnacle, that's the Napes Needle. Any other pinnacle is a pinnacle insofar as it resembles this one: and as it differs from the Napes, by so much is it something other than pinnacle. The Old Man of Hoy has horizontal sandstone bedding; the Old Man of Storr is undercut like a pine-cone. They are pinnacles, but they would be more pinnacular with the rising line and two perched blocks of the Napes one. Those in foreign parts such as Yosemite or the Alps may be taller than the Napes: they are, accordingly, too tall. In 1909, George Abraham spotted a picture of the Napes Needle being sold 'surreptitiously' as a post-card at Chamonix, under the alias of the 'Aiguille du Nuque'. Abraham doesn't say so, but the postcard was presumably a pirated version of his own famous pho-tograph.

So if you're looking for the point of it, look at the Napes Needle. It is, quite simply, the abode of angels, who want to see how many can dance simultaneously on the small summit platform. It is the rock that reaches towards heaven, confounding Aristotle who said stones belong at the centre of the earth, which is why they so constantly strive in the downward direc-tion.

Thus when, in 1992, a group of Peak District climbers wanted an act of ultimate anarchy, they plotted to blow off, with dynamite, the top block of Napes Needle. This would have been a uniquely effec-tive way of enraging Lakeland climbers. Not only is the Needle the icon of the Fell and Rock Climbing Club, but the removal of the top would downgrade the climb from Severe to a negligible Diff. Happily, the Peaklanders couldn't work out how to do it without themselves being destroyed by the fragments crashing down Needle Gully.

Futile it may be to hunt for needles on Haystacks; but Great Gable is remarkably rich in the things. So slog up the steep-ended Gavel Neese, where the first pointy object is Moses Finger. It's named for a smuggler of contraband carbon, for more on whom see Chapter 8.

There is absolutely no evidence that the boulder was originally named for some different, but equally pointy, part of Moses' anatomy—but one can't help wondering anyway. One wouldn't speculate thus on Gladstone's Finger: Gladstone, being a respectable Victorian-era prime minister, was most infrequently to be viewed without his lower garments. But Moses lived in the erotic eighteenth century.

Consider, after all, the evidently Freudian overtones of the Bishop on Barf, above Bassenthwaite Lake. Bishop, indeed! The legend has it that a newly appointed Bishop of Derry, passing this way in 1782, stopped at the Swan Inn and after a few beers got involved in an argument as to whether one could ascend the southern ridge of Barf on one's pack-pony. The Bishop wagered that one could; the white-painted stone marks the high point of his attempt; the other white-painted stone, called the Clerk, marks where he and the horse fell down to, and where their bodies are supposedly buried.

No Roman Catholic bishop of Derry was appointed, or died, in 1782. I've been unable to exclude an Anglican bishop, and I'm told that the bishops of that era were prone to such light-hearted acts. But the story doesn't need researches to rubbish it. The stone's shafted, knob-topped shape suggests a religion older and less sublimated than Christianity. The tradition of anointing this sacred lingam, this natural phallus, surely goes back into antiquity, the white paint being a sanitised Victorian version of a messier and more personal fluid.

It's the roundedness of Moses Finger that qualifies it to stand as Gable's representative of the phallic tendency. But as it's actually a mere perched boulder we'll rest our backs against it for a minute or two, admire its Wasdale view, and head on up.

The White Napes has, according to Wainwright, no notable crags and little of interest. Is it possible that he didn't actually go there? His route up Gavel Neese diverts into Little Hell Gate, a route so continuously gruesome ('a shifting torrent of stones up which palsied limbs must be forced') as to actually be rather appealing. Little Hell Gate is, accordingly, Chapter 15.

The White Napes is forbiddingly steep, until you get on it. And then you find little grassy ramps running up between boulders of clean and grippy rock. Not least among its pleasures is its sideways view of the steep ridges of the Napes, and of the Sphinx and Needle matching one another, rather as Yewbarrow matches Gable at the head of Wasdale.

The Sphinx is sculptural. If it had been carved by human hand, critics would slam it as sentimental and old-fashioned, because its artistic statement is so simply expressed. The Sphinx is also called the Cat, depending on where you're at. It once had, seen from the east, a short tail, a useful foothold for intending climbers. But either name seems appropriate as it looks down disdainfully on your efforts to overcome the short, easy scramble off the Screes Path down into Little Hell Gate.

Pinnacles phallic: pinnacles fanciful. The pinnacle in Great Hell Gate deviates from the Napes ideal in the direction of being perilous and sublime. When the Alps came into fashion, the illustrated papers saved money by sending their engravers, not to Chamonix,

Great Hell Gate Pillar: pinnacle perilous

but to the Shamrock of Ennerdale. Scenery was at its finest when frightening, so the Ennerdale Shamrock would be shown at the moment of being struck by lightning, with bits dropping off to crush the adventurous onlooker.

Sketching the Hell Gate Pillar would be just as sublime, but rather more inconvenient, as the easel isn't going to stay upright in the shifting screes.

From the sublime to the ridiculous is but a single step, said Thomas Paine—adding that back again was equally easy. From Hell Gate Pillar to the Bottle-

18

Shaped Pinnacle is somewhat further, involving a trip halfway round the hill. Spot the Bottle from the small path (Route 9A) under Gable Crag.

Mountains on the whole are rounded and knobby, with crag breaking out here and there. But when we want the ultimate in mountain landscape, we put in a pinnacle.

ROUTE 3 Breast Path

Start: Wasdale Head
Distance to summit: 4½km (3 miles)
Total ascent: 820m (2,700ft)
Terrain: Good paths all the way.

How good? Same Wasdale view all the way, so not quite so good as the Borrowdale version.

> *There is a route up here from Styhead to the summit; it begins over 500 or 600 feet of steep and heavy grass without a path; the rest of the way up is a mixed grill, with a path coming and going.*
> H H Symonds, *Walking in the Lake District,* 1933

From Wasdale Head Hotel, head upstream to the right of Lingmell Beck. After 200 metres, fork off right on a smaller path. The path runs alongside the stream to the long footbridge over Gable Beck. After another 200 metres it bears up left. It is wide and well-built as it slants up the face of Bursting Knott to Sty Head Pass.

At the stretcher box turn left, straight uphill, on a rebuilt stone-surfaced path. Inconspicuous it may have been in 1933, but by the 1960s it was an eroded horror, 50 metres wide, and said to have been visible from space. The National Trust rebuilt it very tidily in 2000. Follow this Breast Path to the summit.

ROUTE 3A Valley route to Sty Head

How good? Much more pleasant, but also much less popular, than the standard route described above. The path, however, is narrow, and in places wet and rough.

After the long footbridge of Gable Beck, continue for 200 metres, then fork right to stay alongside (to the left of) Lingmell Beck. As the ground steepens, look out for a few cairns marking the path. The stream rises to a grassy plateau below Sty Head. Here a wide, green, old path zigzags up to the left, to rejoin the main path 20 metres on the Wasdale side of the Sty Head stretcher box.

3 Fellrunning

A funny sort of fun

Here's a secret. Hillrunners do not actually run uphill.

It's not that it can't be done. A walker who finds the Breast Path, say, a lot of hard work when walking, could start going out for runs on some local moorland, engaging in the (not particularly enjoyable) activity called 'hill reps'. This means finding a short sharp hill, running up it until the anguish is absolutely unbearable, then walking down it (to save the joints) and running up it again. And again. After ten or twelve weeks of this, that ex-walker would be able to run all the way up the Breast Path. The heart, the lungs, and the legs, just grow.

Even so, in an actual fell race, you don't run uphill. This is not just to save some energy for the descents, and even for the brief flat bits. Rather it's because, if you do run (necessarily rather slowly) up the Breast Path, then cannier runners who, with hands on knees and powerful upward strides, are walking up the Breast Path, will—most embarrassingly—overtake you.

Some fellrunners will say that the Borrowdale Race, with its uphill walking, its rich variety of surface underfoot, is actually easier than the same 17 miles along a tarred road. That is a bold paradox, especially given the way the Borrowdale Race starts off. Lightweight studded fell shoes, no load, and over-developed ankles mean that fellrunners have a somewhat frivolous attitude to fell terrain. The race sets off from Stonethwaite Bridge towards Bessyboot—in a straight line. That straight line runs (or, rather, walks with hands on knees) up through a wood at an angle of approximately the roof of a house—a roof on which all the slates are loose and only held together with a few tree roots. (Someone did eventually get hurt, and they've found an alternative start. Tiresome, as it invalidated all the existing race records.)

As a fellrunner, I react to another fellrunner in front in the same way as an untrained dog reacts to a sheep. I can't help but chase after. The excitement of the occasion was enough to get me up the loose stones and on the grassy summit of Bessyboot; 400m of height gained in far too quick a time to get tired. But, after that, it was a case of head into the wind, cloud all around, and a dim runner ahead to follow. Fellrunners only visit summits when the summits have someone on them with a clipboard. Accordingly, the dim runner ahead is skirting the Langstrath side of Glaramara and Allen Crags. And if I lose that dim runner, I might have to stop and look at the map, and that would lose me several seconds.

At Esk Hause the race briefly visits a damp man with a clipboard, then makes its way over the boulders towards Scafell Pike. Rain and buffeting winds make those Scafell boulders awkward. Fellrunning shoes with their soft rubber studs grip like glue on wet grass, but are less good on wet rounded rocks; and fellrunning ankles are scarily exposed. Scafell Pike has another waterproofed person to be ticked off by, and then it's down the Corridor Path to Sty Head, and away up that Breast Path.

Maybe 17 miles of hill really are easier than 17 miles of road. For as I joined the strong-striding line up the Breast Path, I was feeling almost relaxed about it. Movement over the boulders had been slow. Before that, I'd been reining-in my excitement above Langstrath, both so as not to overtake the dim guide ahead (and so have to become a dim guide myself), and also because of being intimidated by a race that was going to have 7,000ft of uphill. Given that one always runs too fast in races, all this moderation meant that I was

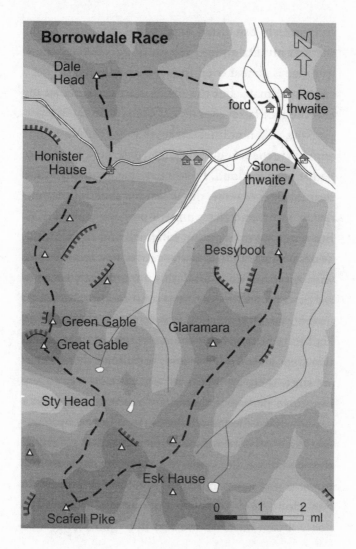

Borrowdale Race

N

Dale Head

Ros-thwaite

ford

Honister Hause

Stone-thwaite

Bessyboot

Green Gable

Glaramara

Great Gable

Sty Head

Esk Hause

Scafell Pike

0   1   2
ml

still scarcely exhausted at all. And once up Gable, there's only Dale Head left to do, 1,200ft at most; this race is almost over! In fact that 7,000ft had been an overestimate: but the slower start certainly let me end the race faster overall…

Now, it's absolutely true that fellrunners don't appreciate the wonderful Borrowdale view. Even if we hadn't been in cloud, I'd still have been looking at the next few feet of scree, the Walsh fell shoes of the runner in front, and that runner's over-large bulgy legs. But while we miss out on Lingmell and the gleam of Wast Water, we do experience the few feet of scree with total intensity. And this applies even more to the descent, where every step must be appraised in an instant, and the scree-slide is felt with the foot and kept in control even as the eye is finding the footfall two steps ahead. All this and, because of that moderate start, there are folk with even tireder legs to slip round, so perhaps I should try a steeper but shorter variant down the loose ledges into Windy Gap.

Down off Green Gable it's soft grass, so grippy to the studded shoe, and just the right angle to lean forward and let wind resistance balance gravity. In grey cloud, and now with nobody else around, is a floaty dream but with the bass-line thump of ground against leg's end. There are cairns, and the path veers off towards Base Brown. But I've a compass handy, and know it's north, so don't waste any seconds messing around with the map. There's a final checkpoint at Honister Hause—don't forget to look both ways on crossing the road—and a delicious plastic cup brimming over with tasty orange liquid composed of Tartrazine, sucrose and a dash of citric acid. Yes, the humble orange squash becomes, after 15 miles of damp hill, a nectar delight.

A timeless time ascending Dale Head in the mist, and down, down, down on a stony path. There's nobody else about, the legs are failing, and this is getting hard. The people ahead are, by definition, faster, so there's no chance of catching anyone. The thought that drives me forward is that the people behind have been taking it easy and are in a state to overtake me. And at last the clouds part to reveal Borrowdale grey under the rain.

There's flat ground along the riverbank, and someone does overtake—I'm useless at flat ground, me. As a final bit of fun there's a ford through the River Derwent to wash off all the mud, only to replace it from the slurry track into the back of Rosthwaite. I've come 114th in a field of 282. And that's triumph, indeed it is, as I sit imbibing even more of the orange nectar and not really having to take my muddy shoes off just yet.

Another few sips of Tartrazine, a shower (the first hundred home probably even got it hot) and a nice cosy car to drive home in. Life, after the Borrowdale Race, is not rich in outward sensation. But it feels just great.

ROUTE 4 Warnscale Bottom

Start:	Gatesgarth Farm pay and display
Distance to summit:	6½km (4 miles)
Total ascent:	850m (2,800ft)
Terrain:	Paths, good for the first ascent, then quite narrow.

How good? Comparatively unchallenging, but enjoyable for the variety of its scenery.

Head up the road for 50 metres towards Honister. On reaching open fell, bear right on the track into Warnscale Bottom. The track reduces to a good, wide path that runs up to the left of the stream. At the gorge top, the path ascends gently towards Dubs Quarry which, with its hut, is seen just ahead; here look out for the smaller, level, path branching right. This leads down to ford Warnscale Beck, then runs up to the right of Little Round How.

Continue along the path for 200 metres, through a dip and up the next rise, then take a fork left, not obvious. The new path runs south and passes to the right of Great Round How, to a stile in a newish fence. Once across the stile, the path runs up to the right of the fence to the Moses Trod path, where you turn right (Route 8, or fork up left to Gillercomb Head and Green Gable).

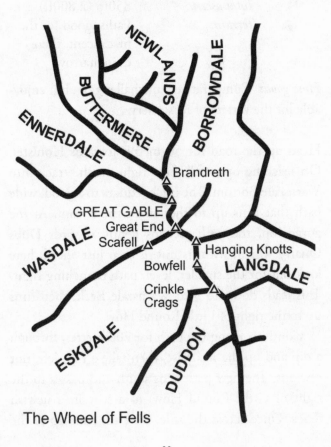

The Wheel of Fells

4 The wheel is real

I know not how to give the reader a distinct image of the country more readily, than by requesting him to place himself with me, in imagination, upon some given point; let it be a cloud hanging midway between Great Gavel, and Scawfell; we shall then see stretched at our feet a number of valleys, not fewer than eight, diverging from the point, on which we are supposed to stand, like spokes from the nave of a wheel.

Wordsworth, *Guide to the Lakes*, 1810

The genteel and literary world came to Great Gable surprisingly late. In 1769, with Skiddaw already a popular ascent, the poet Thomas Gray could write that the passage of Sty Head was 'barred to prying mortals ... a dreadful road' but perhaps possible for a month or two in the summer, given a spell of settled weather and a competent guide. (Meanwhile, quarrymen were packing their ponies across the high face of Great Gable to Wasdale, and Moses Rigg was storing smuggled plumbago in his hut 100m below the summit.)

Early travellers used the coach road that is now the A591 across Dunmail Raise. They found a week's visit as much as their nerves and their legs could stand, and more than enough to fill up a best-selling guide-book; and they went away without even discovering Wasdale, let alone the Esk. Even the early mapmakers, although aware of the pony routes through the hills, failed to name Gable. Presumably they didn't realise that the pointy peak above Wasdale Head was the same as the rounded hump behind Seathwaite, not to mention the double hump visible from the foot (but not the head) of Buttermere.

Great Gable, including the fell top, was perfectly familiar to the shepherds living at its foot. They informed Wordsworth not only of the small pool in the summit rocks, but that that pool never drained dry. There's no grass up there, but should your sheep be in Ennerdale then the top of Gable Crag is the place to stand and see them all at once.

Thus, when Gable first hit print in 1810, it was as a familiar fell that needed no explaining. In the opening pages of Wordsworth's Guide, Gable's right there, acting as the hub for the 'wheel of the dales'. The eight main valleys diverge like spokes from a point on or immediately adjacent to Great Gable.

Gray and his contemporaries decorated Borrowdale with brigands and deadly avalanches. Wordsworth's strength as a guidebook writer is in looking not into his own imagination but outwards, at the real Lakeland. And, consequently, he sees things that are actually there. The radial pattern is not something imposed by the eye (in the way that the astronomer Robert Lowell saw non-existent canals running across the face of Mars). The pattern is actually present on the land.

That pattern breaks as we cross Dunmail Raise: the hills of the east are arranged along two north-south ridges. But of the eight western dales, four do indeed diverge from somewhere on Great Gable, with Eskdale's Hause only two miles away to the east. Three miles away, Rossett Gill is the top end of Langdale. The Duddon springs from a point five miles away, but this is reduced to Ore Gap (three miles) if we mentally undo the capture of Lingcove Beck by the Esk and direct it on its original course down Mosedale.

Wordsworth's eighth vale, Newlands, doesn't run right up to the Gable hub. But even so, it matches the other seven in running directly towards that central point.

This regular arrangement is rather odd. The rocks of Lakeland were formed when Scotland collided with England during the Devonian era. Since then, they've been cracked and broken in every direction. We'd expect the streams, and consequently the valleys, to zigzag and jiggle along the underlying fault-lines. One such fault is defined by the Great Napes face and runs from there south-east. It forms the uphill slash of Skew Gill, and the steep face of Great End. It then runs through the lower col of Esk Hause, the one with the stone shelter cairn. It continues down the gentle valley to Angle Tarn, shows itself clearly in the gully of Rossett Gill, and runs out along Mickleden.

Logically, then, the east side of Gable ought to drain into Langdale. But the streams of Great End, Esk Pike and Hanging Knotts flow across the fault-line into Borrowdale and Langstrath; only at the approach to Langdale is the natural crack also the water course.

The faults and folding of Lakeland's rocks run from north-east to south-west. In Scotland, the valleys and rivers mostly follow this folding—just take a glance at the OS Road Map Sheet 2. In Lakeland, the valleys and rivers follow Wordsworth. The reason for all this is simple, but strange. Lakeland's valleys and rivers are older than Lakeland's hills and ridges.

During long ages after the Devonian, the mountain rocks we now call Borrowdale Volcanics erode right down to ground level and then are flooded by the sea. Shelled creatures live and die, and deposit several thousand metres of limestone on Lakeland.

Some geological eras go by. Lakeland rises slightly out of the sea, and drifts north across the equator. Desert sand blows over, forming several thousand metres of sandstone on top of the lime.

Nothing much happens. A dinosaur wanders by, then nothing much happens. Several more geological eras pass. The continents wheel and shift, and eventually the top left corner of Africa crashes into the bottom-left corner of Europe. Far-away Britain creases up—the Pennines rise as a long ridge, and Cumbria comes up as a dome.

The dome is sandstone and limestone, and knows nothing of the ancient Caledonian chain underneath. Streams run straight outwards from the middle, in a pattern of 'radial drainage'. The streams deepen, become rivers. The rivers carve themselves valleys, and cart away an inch or two of the sandstone, then another inch, and eventually all of it. And then the rivers cart away the limestone. A purple boulder emerges: a small mouse-like creature patters across it. Over the next 100 million years or so, the river system simply sinks, like a hot griddle lying on an ice cream. Borrowdale finally gets down into the Borrowdale Volcanics.

At the very moment when the grey-purple dome hasn't in its turn eroded down to sea level, the world goes cold and some glaciers carve big interesting hollows into it. Between three glacier hollows stands a tiny platform of what was the top of the grey-purple dome. It's Great Gable—but it won't be great for long. Some humans wander past, in a brief warm period,* then become extinct. The ice-valleys enlarge, chew away all of the intervening hills. Cumbria is level once again: Lakeland is a blob where the bedrock is dark rather than sandy or lime.

The River Derwent, now flowing through grey Lakeland rocks, originally ran through sandstone 2,000m higher up. Today, the sea-bottom rocks have gone from high Lakeland—you can still see them round the edges (there's sandstone at St Bees, limestone at Moor Divock). But the ancient valleys are still there, in their wheel-spoke pattern, centred on Great Gable.

*The asterisk marks the point in the paragraph we currently call 'the present'.

ROUTE 5 Warnscale Beck

Start:	Gatesgarth Farm pay and display
Distance to summit:	7½km (4½ miles)
Total ascent:	900m (3,000ft)
Terrain:	Gill scramble Grade 1.

How good? This is a long, scenic and interesting stream scramble, where all difficulties can be avoided at will.

Head up the road for 50 metres, then bear right on the track into Warnscale Bottom. Where it passes between two stones, the main path (Route 4) continues ahead, to the left of the stream. This scramble option will go up the stream itself. The description is bottom to top, ie against the water flow. The stream line runs up with several small waterfalls, then runs up to the right as a cascade, to bend sharply back left in a small gorge. Just above this zigzag, a steeper rocky area of the slope has (usually) two waterfalls side by side. Above the rock band, the stream runs across left in an open gorge, not steep.

Just after the two stones, bear right on a faint grass path to cross a footbridge. Follow the grass path ahead, across Black Beck, and up to the right of Warnscale Beck. As the path steepens, bear left to join the stream at its first small waterfall. Mossy slabs to the left of this fall are followed by bare rock to the left of the stream, past a second fall.

The third fall drops into the disconformity pool (see the main chapter below). Step across the stream, and climb the chunky rock to the right of the fall on good holds. Continue on bare rock beside the stream, to the long cascade that slants up to the right. This has pleasant rock to its right all the way up. At its top, the stream turns sharp left into the small gorge, with a handsome but not climbable fall in the darkness at its head. So come out of the ravine and go up its left-hand rim on gentle slabs, to the fall's top.

Here the ravine kinks sharply right. Go into it, dodging under a tree, and taking to a ledge on the right-hand wall. From the ledge, climb up steeply on good holds, out of the ravine. Go up the ravine rim to the foot of the rock band with the two waterfalls.

Cross left to a wooded platform below the rock band and go up the island area between the two streams. Cross the stream on the left, then return to the island area near its top, to finish by a brief rocky arête.

Above the rock band, walk up rocks to the left of the recombined stream to where it bends left into the gentle open gorge. This gives bouldery walking to a waterfall. The foot of this can be reached by an awkward step on the right wall just above the water (or avoided up left). The fall itself has some good scrambling to its right on small splintery holds. After more bouldery walking, a little V-fall has a delicate wall on its left, again avoidable by a detour up the left wall. Soon you reach the gorge top, where the stream arrives down the left-hand wall in a splashy fall. Short of the fall by about 20 metres, head up the steep left-hand wall: just to the left of a tiny stream trickle there

Grade 1 scrambling in Warnscale Beck

is a line of large holds, a fine finish to arrive on the main path (Route 4) above.

The good path runs up to the left of the stream. As it ascends gently towards Dubs Quarry (with its hut) seen ahead, look out for the smaller path branching right. This leads down to ford Warnscale Beck, then runs up to the right of Little Round How. This rock knoll gives a short Grade 1 scramble on good rock, starting from the path.

Continue along the path for 200 metres, through a dip and up the next rise, then take a fork left, not obvious. The new path runs south and passes to the right of Great Round How, to a stile in a newish fence. You can continue as Route 4, above, but for extra scrambling, don't cross the stile. Instead, head along the fence to its corner and then ahead, slanting up to join a cairned small path. Turn left, contouring to join a larger path descending from above right but running level ahead. (You are briefly reversing Moses Trod, Route 8.)

Above the path, the face of Grey Knotts is gentle grass with various small outcrops sticking out. Link several of these for a scrambly way up. At the summit switch into Route 9 (Grey Knotts and Green Gable).

5 Volcanoes and underwater sludge

*What Gable's made of: examining by
scrambling the Borrowdale Volcanics*

Long, long ago, and somewhere in the southern hemi-
sphere, something that would later be called Scotland
crashed into what is now known as England. Off the
shore of 'England' stood a chain of volcanic islands,
composed of crunchy grey lava. In a deep ocean trench
between the islands and the arriving 'Scotland' lay
grit, sand and sludge. As the continents collided, the
ocean sludge was crushed, compressed, and squeezed
up against the lumpy lava, to make a mountain chain
of maybe 8,000m in height.

Those mountains were worn down to sea level
before even the dinosaurs could tramp their glaciers
and admire the view of the coal swamps. But much,
much later, as Africa crashed into Spain at the other
end of Europe, the stumps of the lost range rose again
to become the Lake District. The rugged lumpy landscape of Great Gable, Helvellyn and the Scafells is
carved out of the crushed remains of the volcanic
islands: their purplish-grey rock is called Borrowdale Volcanic. The one-time ocean muds and sludges
make the northern hills: this is the Skiddaw Slate.

Look back along Buttermere and you can see them both.

The Skiddaw Slate is smooth and slightly shiny, a bit like pencil lead. It's slippery when you stand on it, and particularly slippery when wet. It breaks down into flat circular pebbles; when you try to build it into summit cairns, the summit cairns fall down. The hills it forms are steep but smooth. Often the crests are sharp and rocky, but the sides hold only small outcrops of crag and long slopes of scree. In the view you see, Grasmoor and Robinson are Skiddaw Slate.

The Borrowdale Volcanic Series is angular, and it does make crags. All Lakeland's rock climbs are on the Volcanics; when you think of real Lakeland scenery, it's the chunky, lumpy landscape of the BVS. And looking down the left-hand side of the valley, that means Haystacks, and High Crag, and High Stile.

In Warnscale Bottom, you can see the two of them where they meet. Look up at Fleetwith Pike. The top of the slope is Striddle Crag: black and broken and speckled with heather. It's the Borrowdale Volcanic. But halfway down, it all changes. The outcrops are small and rounded; the ground between is steep but gentle grass. It's the Skiddaw Slate. The dividing line rises gently to the left, and crosses the ridge-line of

Fleetwith Edge. Walkers coming down that edge in Chapter 6, especially if in the wet, will notice the sudden slipperiness as they step across that line.

So what we're standing on, at valley bottom, is Skiddaw Slate. The best place to see it nice and clean, with the weathered surface stripped away, is in the bed of the beck. And the best way to see the junction line between the two sorts of stone will be to follow the beck all the way up. Which will also, if the water's not too high, give some great Grade 1 scrambling.

The scrambling is good. So good that, aiming eagerly upwards, I entered the pool basin on grey Lakeland rock, clambered over some more grey Lakeland to exit, and had already done the next cascade before I realised what I'd missed. I had stepped across several million years of geology without even noticing.

So I backtracked, and poked around. The approach below the pool is grey Lakeland with a texture like flaky pastry rolled out by someone with a very dirty rolling pin. The pool's downhill rim is similar, but set on edge: it's like jammed-together pages of an old and decomposing book. (As indeed it is: the book is 200 million years old, with little dead graptolites trapped between the pages.) But at the uphill side, between the two rowan trees, the Lakeland grey is smooth and solid, with shadows of reddish-orange, and green. It's not obvious if you're not in the habit of looking at lava. But wander around, and in a minute or two you become aware of the difference between the lower rim, which is the Skiddaw Slate, and the top, which is a lava of the Borrowdale Volcanic. And outwards from the pool's left corner, you can trace the junction line around the hill to where it runs along the foot of Striddle Crags.

The two rowan trees, and the hollow of the pool, and the mossed rocks: this is a place to hang around and let the spray from the waterfall soak into the soul. If there are people on the paths alongside you can't see them; and the waterfall is noisy enough that you can't hear them either. For me, the rowan was bare, and the waterfall at the pool's back ran under ice. But equally, let the rowan be in new leaf (and I bet there are primroses then); or let it be in acrid flower; or let it be red with berries, and the bracken just dying on the slopes. Buttermere gleams down-valley: up-valley is an impressive bleakness of bare rock, with the heathery gloom of Haystacks impending on the right.

But maybe it's a grey drizzly day when you don't want to linger, and listen to the waters, and gradually discern the subtle textural difference between the grey slate and the grey lava. Well, on just those days Nature has offered a short cut. Simply scramble the good lava immediately to the right of the falls, and notice how wet lava is still crisp and climbable, as against the slippery damp slate lower down.

And then scramble onwards and upwards, by waterfalls and small gorges. Where the lava came straight out of the crater it forms rough mossy slabs, and breaks into big footholds. Where volcanic ash fell from the sky in piles, the consequent rock is called tuff; it's grainy and textured, breaking into small but sharp handholds. And at Little Round How, it's lava underwater, swirled and slumped. Scramble that as well.

The Borrowdale Volcanics. Formed 200 million years ago for your scrambling pleasure. If you haven't had enough of it by Round How, you can head sideways and find some more on Grey Knotts.

Note: If it's not enough to scramble up the BVS, you could also, until very recently, sleep inside it. High on the face above Warnscale Bottom stands a small quarryman's hut, its walls made of BVS blocks, its roof of Honister slate (which, despite the name, is a compressed form of BVS as well). The hut was famous for its tin box and Bible, its tiny window with the big, big view of Buttermere. Early in 2005 it suffered a bizarre accident. A thoughtless hut-lover cached a spare cylinder of gas inside the hut's chimney. The next visitors brought no camping stove but did bring coal, newspaper and sticks for a living fire. In the midnight explosion they were, happily, uninjured: but the hut's roof was blown off. The Dubs quarry hut, at NY209134, is less romantic but will at least keep the rain out.

Warnscale Head bothy, before losing its roof

ROUTE 6 Fleetwith Pike

Start:	Gatesgarth
Distance to summit:	6½km (4 miles)
Total ascent:	1,000m (3,300ft)
Terrain:	Paths, steep on the upper ridge.

How good? Fleetwith Edge is a fine little ridge, and the views back along Buttermere are outstanding. As a descent route it's rather arduous, but you get the full benefit of those views.

The spur of Fleetwith Pike rises from the car park, but the foot of it is steep broken ground marked by a memorial cross. To avoid this, head up the road towards Honister for 300 metres, then fork right at a public-footpath signpost. A clear path zigzags up the flank of the spur to reach its top above the steep ground. (If reversing this route, look out for a tall cairn at this point.)

The sharp ridge rises gently to 450m altitude, where it steepens with short rocky steps: not real scrambling, but an occasional handhold will be taken. The first of the steps is on slippery Skiddaw Slate, but then the underlying rock changes to Borrowdale Volcanic, which, though just as steep, is rough and gives good grip. The spur arrives quite suddenly at the summit of Fleetwith Pike.

A path runs west along the top of Honister Crag, dropping gently past disused quarries to the embankment at the top of the old tramway. Cross this, and continue as Route 8 (Moses Trod) to Gillercomb Head and Green Gable, or to Beck Head.

6 Death and the maiden

Gt. Gable ... summit was dismal today. 'Too many people getting their ashes dropped around here these days,' I said pointing at the obvious debris from the containers of aged fell-walkers' remains: 'Looks like the floor of a bonemeal factory,' said Ken, and turned for my special descent route into Windy Gap.

Joss Naylor, on his record-breaking run in 1987 over all the Wainwrights, from *Joss Naylor MBE Was Here*

Among the crags at the foot of Fleetwith Pike stands a white-painted stone cross, visible from a mile away along the Buttermere shore. The death that it commemorates happened over a hundred years ago; it is a rare example of an accident caused by faulty alpenstock technique.

The alpenstock (alpine stick) was made of stout ashwood, a couple of feet longer than the modern walking pole, with a spiked toe and adze-and-pick head like the modern ice-axe. In the 1880s it was carried as a mountaineering accessory even in summer.

There was, it seems, a technique of descending broken ground by leaning over each small crag, planting the spike in the grass below it, and then sliding down the stick. The unfortunate Miss Fanny Mercer hadn't been properly instructed. She didn't slide her hands down the stick.

People who have fallen over crags and surprisingly survived tell us that the process is actually not all that frightening. Their testimony suggests that poor Miss Mercer may have thought something like, 'Good Heavens, that was rather silly of me!' as she pole-vaulted into space; her eye would even have registered the chimneypots of Gatesgarth immediately below, and the celebrated view all along Buttermere that she was falling into.

Even today death is a part, albeit a small part, of the fellwalking life. In an average year, nineteen people die in the Lakeland fells. Of these, thirteen are fellwalkers. (The remainder comprise one rock climber, four described as 'not mountain accidents', with the final unfortunate being a scrambler, ice climber or fellrunner. Lake District Search and Mountain Rescue Association figures, 1991–2004.) Given the number of people on the fells, this is a fairly small figure. The average UK resident spends 0.2 days a year walking in Lakeland, and dies once every 75 years, so we'd expect about 400 deaths a year, from natural causes alone, to take place during such visits. We have to conclude that far too few people are dying in the hills. (Which just shows the danger in simple statistics. In fact we tend to go up Great Gable on days when we're not feeling poorly. We tend to die on days when we are.)

Are you more likely to get killed fellwalking than driving home afterwards on the M6? There are twenty million visits to Lakeland each year. Assume that half are for fellwalking, rather than shopping, sipping tea, and visiting Beatrix Potter at Sawrey, and that each involves 200 miles of car travel. UK road travel is about 10,000 miles per person per year, and this results in ten road deaths per day. The outcome is about twelve road deaths annually while travelling to or from the Lakes. That figure's approximate: a mile of M6 is safer than a random road mile, but a tired driver is less safe than a random driver. Still, it does suggest that going up Great Gable is roughly as dangerous as driving home to Manchester.

We do have an internal alarm system to warn us against situations where we're liable to die. It's called fear. And it works well when we're confronted with a snake, or a large scowling human, or Honister Crag. Nasty chemicals flood into our brains and we jump backwards or edge warily away.

However, there's an override. If we see others sliding down their alpenstocks and surviving, we feel less scared ourselves. And once we've achieved four or five exposed scrambles like the Napes Traverse, and if we're still alive afterwards, we stop worrying.

This is not rational. The fact that we've survived five times out of five merely indicates that the odds of death are probably lower than 20 per cent. Surviving five scrambles implies only that scrambling is at least as safe as playing Russian Roulette. Of course it may be less dangerous than that: but our experience so far simply doesn't supply useful evidence.

Ah, but I can see lots of other people doing it, so it must be okay? That is the other mistake in our built-in fear programming. At a French resort where I was skiing, someone lifted a safety tape and ventured off into the fresh powder. That the person wanted the fresh powder makes him an experienced skier, so it must have been knowingly that he took a certain risk for the pleasure of the powder. He was unlucky. That particular powder had a cliff below; he skied over it and was killed.

The really sad part happened ten minutes later. Another skier saw the tracks running under the safety tape, followed them down, and skied over the same cliff.

Scrambling is less safe than simple fellwalking; it is also less safe than roped rock climbing. On Blencathra on a day of frozen paths and chilled fingers I watched a helicopter lift someone from below Sharp Edge; and, because the victim had not been given a helmet, realised that he was no longer alive. So, using primitive statistics, I have always known that scrambling is lethal. I was surprised to find, from those Lake District Mountain Rescue figures above, that between 1993 and 2004 just three scrambling fatalities were recorded. For me, a day without scrambling is like Kendal mint cake without the cake. And I'll even brave the dangers of the M6, just to get to Great Gable.

When we do fall off the Napes Traverse or Fleetwith Edge, we shall at least cease to be a footpath problem to the National Park. But your descendants, they plaque you up. In the 1880s, a 5ft white cross was the obvious answer. Today, that would be considered a bit too intrusive—you can see the thing from the other end of Buttermere.

The first recorded person to die on Striding Edge was Mr Gough, in 1805. His small dog guarded his body for several months, and was turned into verse by Wordsworth and by Sir Walter Scott. Gough himself is commemorated by a pointed cairn at the top of the ridge. The second victim was Mr Dixon, following the foxhounds in 1858. His memorial is a sort of metal plaque on a stand. But now many a tiny top in the Lake District has its brass plate and plastic flower.

In the Tatras mountains of Slovakia they've found a solution. Put all the plaques on one little hill—a pretty hill, with cedars and tumbled boulders. Put the yellow-flashed trail through the middle and charge the punters ten crowns. They call it the symbolic cemetery (*symbolicky cintorin*). It is—can we call it fun? I think we can. It has crucifixes painted to look like totem poles, bas-reliefs in copper of the fatal avalanche, aluminium eagles ascending to heaven or at least to the summit of Gerlachovsky Stit. The place is filling up: to get in these days, you not only have to die in the hills but do something useful for them while still alive.

Copper plaques and graveyard flowers aren't quite on a par with other forms of litter. I wouldn't urge fellwalkers to remove them—apart from the cellophane wrappers, which should certainly be taken down off the hill. But I do invite fellwalkers not to leave them in the first place.

On a recent ascent of Harrison Stickle, I noticed on the last ledges below the cairn a pale-coloured grit or gravel that didn't seem to belong to the surrounding tuffs and lavas. It was, I realised after I'd scrambled through it, somebody's ashes.

Given that Gable summit is probably the UK's most popular ash-scatter spot, some thought does have to be given to the effect on the mountain. On Cairn Gorm, the rangers are slightly anxious about the mineral-rich material altering the natural plant life; their advice is scatter the stuff properly, and not leave your departed friend lying about in little heaps. And do you really want your ashes scrambled through by me on my way up Harrison Stickle, or ending up inside Joss Naylor's running shoes? A friend on the Cobbler on a breezy day found a gritty material blowing into his sandwiches. Yes, he'd eaten several bites of cheese 'n' deceased before he realised...

ROUTE 7 Ennerdale

Start:	Gatesgarth, Buttermere valley
Distance to summit:	6½km (4 miles)
Total ascent:	900m (3,000ft)
Terrain:	Good paths, until the final scree-boulder climb from Beck Head.

How good? Upper Ennerdale is grassy and not very spectacular, but it does provide an unusual and remote approach.

Directly opposite the car park, a narrow gate beside the farmyard is signed 'Lakeside Path'. Pass the farm to a wider track, then ignore a left fork. The wide path crosses the valley floor to Peggy's Bridge, and zigzags up right and then, at the corner of a plantation, back left. It slants quite gently up to Scarth Gap, where an inconspicuous path turns off right, up High Crag, and a much more obvious one turns left to Haystacks.

The path runs down ahead, to the left of felled plantation, to a track with a gate. Turn left, away from the gate, to pass the erratic boulder and *roche moutonnée* described below, and reach Black Sail Hut.

Here the path turns slightly right, to a footbridge over the River Liza, and heads up among drumlins (also described below) towards Black Sail Pass. The path joins Sail Beck and goes up to the right of it. As the path turns sharply away from Sail Beck, cross the stream and go up grassy slopes on its left for 100 metres to immediately below where the beck becomes a small gorge. Here you find the Kirk Fell Contour Path, and turn left along it.

The path is narrow, with occasional cairns. As it passes above Boat How outcrop, it fades away, but keep on the same level and look out for cairns to rediscover it. It then climbs very gently around the hill, to arrive at the lowest point of the Beck Head saddle, beside the iron posts of a former gateway.

Turn left across the saddle, and take the obvious path (Route 1) up Gable's steep north-west spur.

7 Ice is nice

The odd thing about a glacier is its ugliness. Not the upper glacier, where it's snow-covered and just looks like snow with a few funny cracks running across it. But the lower glacier, the dry glacier as it's called, where the ice is bare.

Ice should be cold. The dry glacier, after you spent half the day walking uphill to reach it, is hot under the afternoon sun. Ice should be sparkly. The dry glacier is dirty grey, with stones lying all over. It has a pile of rubble along either side, where rock has fallen from the crags and then crept slowly down-valley on its icy conveyor. And if two glaciers have joined, the rubble along their joining edges is now a rubble-stripe down the middle.

The dry glacier, above all, ought to be dry. In fact, under the afternoon sun, it runs with water. Little streams babble along between banks of ice. Those banks are rounded like underground limestone, but forming and reforming in hours rather than geological ages. The streams hold particles of ice, and particles of grit, and are dirty grey like the ice they run through.

Wet feet and stream crossings are, accordingly, a problem. Crossing the unstable rubble to get on the ice in the first place is a problem. But the main problem comes with the crevasses. Ice is very solid. Where it goes round a bend, it cracks on the outer side of the curve. Where it hauls itself over a hump, it cracks right across. And where it comes to a steepening, it breaks into chunks, from house-size to airport-terminal-size, and falls over the edge one chunk at a time.

The beauty lies in the detail. A stream comes to a crevasse and falls in: the hole gets worn by falling water but also shrunk down by refrozen splashes and so forms a twisty curve, as your intestine would be if you happened to be a snowman with innards made of ice. Down inside the glacier the stream chuckles and shouts: it's called *moulin de glacier* or glacier waterwheel.

Again, water gathers in a pothole pool. The pool is circular and expands below the surface like a green eye. It's the *marmite de glacier*, the ice-cauldron. A boulder stands high above the glacier, on a toadstool stalk of ice that the boulder itself has protected from the sun.

The crevasses: green in their depths, blue in their even deeper depths, and a sudden chill from below as you leap across in your crampons. Two crevasses converge, leaving a blade of sun-shrunken transparent ice: very pretty, unless you were trying to cross the glacier between those two particular crevasses.

From above, the glacier looked like a wide smooth road running up among the mountains. When you're on it, it's a road of sorts, but one supplied with booby traps, tollbooths, and site-specific sculpture.

Lakeland is a glacier landscape. We happen to be in a warm spell—one that's been running for a mere 10,000 years and could end at any time. But even in their absence, we can read the landscape in a language of glaciers. That language is simple and brutal. The ice elbows its way down Ennerdale with a grunt and a shove, and with a martial-arts screech slices off the end of Angler's Crag.

You can pick up the basics of this language in an afternoon crossing Ennerdale. Go on to study it over all Lakeland, and even take a native-speaker trip to the actual glaciers of the Alps, and you'll be reading the scenery with some fluency. For the graduate course you'll need to lie under blizzard snows for a few thousand years, until the meltwater flows below your slow white tongue and you actually start to speak in Icekimo.

The insight that this country has recently been under ice is so satisfying because it accounts for so many different things. Streams make steep little slot valleys; but glaciers barge through the scenery like an elephant in a shopping mall. And so the Buttermere valley is U-profile, flat-bottomed and steep-sided. Ice isn't elastic. Coming down off Brandreth and Grey Knotts it can't level off all at once; but keeps on going down, before it can turn uphill again. And that leaves a hole, waiting to be filled with water: so that we now have a Lake District rather than a District of Rather Rocky Grassy Bits.

On the path down from Scarth Gap, recent felling on your right shows the U-shaped profile of Ennerdale. You can also now see Ennerdale Water. From the left, Angler's Crag sticks into the lake. It looks as if it was meaning to wander on bumpily to the right, for maybe another half mile, until the glacier chopped off its bottom end. Such 'truncated spurs' are the equivalent of the bloodstained bludgeon: this landscape has been assaulted by ice.

The clearing of that wood pulp plantation also reveals the top of Pillar Rock against the skyline opposite.

The path drops to a track, running left towards

the youth hostel. Perched on the left is a boulder the size of a small garden shed. As Chairman Mao didn't quite say: 'Where do large boulders come from? Do they fall from the sky? No.' Well this one, at any rate, is no meteorite, as it's made of good grey Lakeland rock. Did it crack off the crags of Haystacks 300m above? But look: you can see sky underneath. It's quite surprising if this hut-like rock has rolled on its supporting stones and come to a stop without crushing them. It's also surprising that the hut-rock didn't fall apart itself, as it is quite cracked. So it's more plausible to read this as a rock fallen on the glacier up-valley, and gently lowered to its present position as the ice melted.

Such boulders are more obviously ice-borne when the valley head has a different sort of stone: and hunks of pink granite from Shap are found as far away as the North Yorks Moors. Sometimes the glacier drops them off not in valley bottoms but perched on the crests of ridges: hence the Hanging Stone on the north ridge of Base Brown (Route 10B). Such lost rocks are called 'erratics', which means wandering.

Some stones fall down into crevasses, and the glacier drags them across the bedrock like fingernails across a slate, at a rate of several centimetres a year and utterly implacably. This is what makes the glacier such an effective piece of earth-carving equipment. And where a knoll or a rock sticks up into the glacier, its top gets scratched right off and its front gets smoothed and scraped, while at its downhill end the ice plucks out boulders like a dentist taking out teeth. All this sounds rather violent and exciting; so you're going to be somewhat disappointed when I stop you, 30 metres after the end of the plantation, to point out a lump of rock in the grass just to the right of the track.

Okay, so its Great Gable end is gently sloping, with a slight hump, and is then gently sloping again. And its Ennerdale end is rather steeper, and perhaps a bit broken up. Does this really show a glacier moving from left to right across it? On any lump of rock, one end has to be steeper than the other. Hmmm—how about if the next lump of rock we come to is also arranged the same way?

The ground hereabouts is covered with conical hillocks, and the next bedrock is a little way away. We pass the youth hostel, and curve down to the wooden footbridge over the Liza. Here, again, the recent felling gives a view of Pillar Rock up against the sky on the right: Pisgah, Jordan Gap, and High Man. But your attention is directed to a rather smaller rock, only 20cm high. As you step off the footbridge it rises immediately in front of you. Smooth and gentle on the left: steep on the right. See?

Geologists have given us the Ordovician and the Silurian, named after two mid-Welsh tribes—even the Romans had trouble remembering which was which. But some earth words are worthy, like the 'clints' and 'grikes' of limestone pavement. And, here, the smooth up-ice side is 'lee'; and the steep, plucked, down-ice side is 'stoss'; and the item entire is *roche moutonnée*. The ice-squashed rock is indeed sheep-shaped, but it actually takes its name from a wig, worn by nine-teenth-century barristers, that was smoothed down with mutton fat.

Perhaps my two examples still haven't convinced you—they constitute two rather smudged finger-prints of the glacier rather than the smoking gun or the bloodstained knuckleduster. However, once you do start seeing sheepified rocks, you see them everywhere. High up the fellside of Kirk Fell, the entire outcrop of Boat How is a sheep-type wig sized for a rather bigger barrister. And Haystacks itself is sheep-shaped, plucked off at its end above Scarth Gap. (If you doubt that ice went right over

Haystacks, wander around up there until you find some erratic boulders. There are convincing ones above Blackbeck Tarn.)

Heading up towards Scarth Gap, direct your investigator's eye at Tongue Gill, which runs down to the left of the long grassy spur called the Tongue at the valley head. Why has this stream formed its V-groove slantwise along the flank of Brandreth? And Loft Beck, as it joins it, is also kinked to the right. These streams have been diverted along the edge of a glacier that isn't there any more.

A more obvious oddity is the multitude of little conical hillocks over the valley floor. Each has a cap of dark heather, showing that the tops are better drained than the bottoms. These are drumlins, with the entire collection called a 'swarm'. They are the remains of the rubble dragged along the glacier's base through its final centuries of soggy collapse. Why does the slushy rubble end up in such neat hillocks? This is something the geologists are still arguing about. Rub your hands together after a day's fellwalking, and the sweaty dirt forms into little neat rolls. The collection of gravel dirt under moving ice could be similar. Each drumlin may have rolled itself up around a single large boulder.

But for Creation Scientists, the drumlins are evidence that the glaciers never actually happened. Those who believe that Lakeland's shapes were formed by Noah's Flood will also have to account for the high little hollows called, locally, coombs (geologically, corries) on the northern and eastern faces of many hills. Great Gable is so crammed with fell features that there wasn't room for a coombe or corrie, but there are fine examples above Buttermere. The Unscientists must also account for hanging valleys like Gillercomb, running out halfway up the side of glacially overdeepened Borrowdale.

A day that starts up Scarth Gap will usually end in Buttermere village. And as you lick your homemade ice cream from the milk of the Buttermere Ayrshires, think of the similar stuff that so recently crept 1,000m high above your head.

ROUTE 8 Moses Trod

Start: Honister Hause
Distance to summit: 4½km (3 miles)
Total ascent: 600m (2,000ft)
Terrain: Small paths, tricky in mist.

How good? Fine situations, with crag above and Ennerdale below.

The tramway leads up west, the path following it at first, then going to its right. At the top, a cairned path sets off on the left. This climbs gently south, then curves south-west around the flank of Brandreth.

You could fork up left to Gillercomb Head, to cross Green Gable to Windy Gap (see Route 9). But for Moses' original route, contour around the north flank of Green Gable below its steep broken face. The path becomes clearer as it arrives in Stone Cove below Windy Gap. (A rather nasty scree path runs up from here to Windy Gap.) Contour on below the screes of Gable Crag, and climb slightly to reach a knoll on Gable's north-west spur (NY208107), 30m above Beck Head. Turn up the steep scree path to the summit plateau.

8 Wadd's it all about?
The carbon heart of Great Gable

Great Gable can be gone up for the views, or for the geology, or for the historic interest. It can be gone up for the scrambling, or for the rock problems, or even for the mountain ringlet butterfly. We don't need any new reasons to go up Gable.

Nevertheless, three outdoor journalists from *Trail* magazine found a good one. Somewhere on the hill once stood probably Britain's earliest (and certainly England's highest) hilltop habitation. Long before the Snowdon café or the Nevis Observatory, before even the sappers' hut on Ben Macdui, the legendary Moses Rigg built a small hut known as the Smugglers' Retreat among the rocks of Gable Crag.

Moses built so as to be hard to find and hard to get to. His hut was used, says legend, for the distillation of illegal whisky, mixed from the bogwaters of Brandreth for a rich brown-golden colour and a taste to challenge the wildest of Scottish island malts. The hut had been last spotted by rock climbers fifty years ago, and was almost fallen down even then. The journalists had chosen a day of thick low cloud for their quest.

But heck—who needs a reason for going up Gable?

Trail rather favours such expressions as 'but heck'. *Trail* has described Gable as 'the new Tryfan'. But *Trail*'s journos (Jeremy Ashcroft and Guy Procter, with photographer Tom Bailey) do know a good story; and one good story is a long-lost smugglers' hut, and dubious ropework on the rain-soaked grass above the crags, and close-up photos of happy wet walkers, and the smugglers' hut in the end still retaining its inscrutable unfindableness. Except that they found it.

And inside, on a small stone shelf undisturbed for a couple of centuries, was a strange slippery stone that left a grey mark when rubbed. What it was all about wasn't whisky. What it was about was wadd.

Wadd, also known as plumbago or blacklead, was between 1700 and 1800 the UK's most precious mineral resource. Armed guards protected it, the miners were body-searched at the end of every shift, and pitched battles with musket and cutlass were fought across the floor of Borrowdale. The trade in stolen wadd that took place in the back rooms of the inns of Keswick was the world's first black market, so called because of the grey stains it left on those who handled it. Today, wadd is familiarly known only as the 'lead' in pencils. It is, in fact, graphite: a crystalline form of pure carbon.

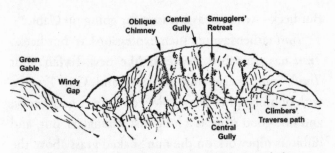

This diagram, from an early 20th-century guidebook, shows the location of the Smugglers' Retreat.

Heat deep underground vaporises various components of the rocks, which then drift upwards and condense in cracks and seams of the rocks higher up. Different materials condense at different places, so that you get a seam of lead, or of copper, or of iron pyrites. The cracking tower in a modern oil refinery works the same way. What is rare and unusual is for organic matter, produced at the earth's surface, to get folded and carried to the depths where this sort of thing can happen. Plumbago is made of reprocessed body-parts from the very dawn of life.

The deposit on the side of Grey Knotts was the first ever found, the purest ever found, and the only one in Britain. It is a strange substance. It's soft enough to be used as a non-greasy lubricant: a grey pencil drawn down the zip of your waterproof jacket makes it run more smoothly. At the same time it's stable up to 3367°C, far above the melting point of any metal. In this lay its military importance. In a mould made of graphite you can cast a perfectly spherical cannonball or musket ball, again and again. The accurate gunnery of Nelson's navy depended on the wadd mines of Seathwaite.

Today we come up Borrowdale to climb Great Gable. In the 1780s, they came up Borrowdale on a sort of geography field trip. (The activity is the same; only the excuses alter through the centuries.) And in the days when going to the summit of Skiddaw was a dangerous and eccentric adventure, the unique mining industry above Seathwaite was an absolute must-see. And it's still well worth a visit today—especially as it can easily be combined with a climb of Gable.

From Seathwaite, you can see, all the way up the slope to the right of Sour Milk Gill, the yellowish heaps of scree spoil from the wadd mines. From the farm, cross the valley and the River Derwent, and turn right across a smaller footbridge. A slab by the path is marked Joseph Banks Esquire, and dated 1752: it indicated his ownership of the valuable mines above.

Not far ahead now are the Borrowdale Yews, celebrated by Wordsworth; but you're after industry not poetry, so turn uphill on a faint old zigzag path to the first of the yellow spoil heaps. Here are the low remains of a stout building, the office of the mine superintendent and also the guard house, from which armed wadd-thieves were driven off with musket fire.

The miners' path winds upwards, past another of Mr Banks' markers, to reach some mine holes high above the valley and alongside a charming little waterfall. It's easy to imagine the miners emerging at the end of an eleven-hour shift, blowing out the tallow candles set on the peaks of their grey-stained sweaty caps, washing their grey faces in the waterfall, and pausing for a moment to enjoy the view down Borrowdale. Inside, the mine hole slopes down steeply to a four-way junction where one of the passages is straight up, letting in a shaft of pearly light and a drift of raindrops, while another is straight down into black depths. In the wall are bolt belays left by the MOLES or Mines of Lakeland Exploration Society: the place offers obvious dangers to the inexperienced without helmets and safety ropes.

The path winds up steeply, past more mines, to a ladder stile over a stone wall where the slope eases into the upper part of Gillercomb. The stile is 100 metres north-east of Newhouse Gill, at NY231127: a useful marker for those seeking the mines from above. From here you can contour left and drop gently into Gillercomb, or head up north-west to join the fence 400 metres north of Grey Knotts' summit.

So what of Moses Rigg and his hut? With armed guards at the valley floor, it made sense to smuggle plumbago upwards. And around the high slope of Gable, a convenient transport route was provided by a completely different mineral industry. From Honister top, around under Gable Crag, and down by Beck Head into Wasdale, ran Moses Trod, also known as Moses Sledgate. Sleds loaded with slate took this

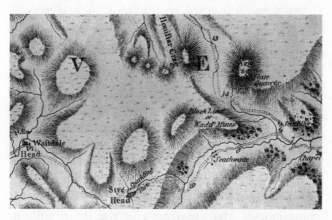

This map of 1774 shows Gable, sort of, but a far more compelling destination is the Borrowdale wadd mine.

ingenious and convenient route out of the mountains towards the ports of Drigg and Ravenglass.

Long before Coleridge had his adventure on the rocks of Scafell, the quarrymen of Honister were abseiling from crag tops with wooden wedges and hammers. From the crags of Fleetwith they brought down the slates in wooden sleds, a quarter-ton at a time. The load came down 1,000ft to Gatesgarthdale Beck in minutes:

> *The long swift steps seem almost to fly; the noise of the crashing slate comes nearer; now we see the man's eager face, and now we hear his panting breath, and now he draws up by the roadside— every muscle strained, every nerve alive, and every pulse throbbing with frightful force. It is a terrible trade—and the men employed in it look wan and worn, as if they were all consumptive or had heart disease.*

The description, from the 1850s, is by Eliza Lynn Linton.

Honister was avoided by respectable folk, especially after dark. The quarry workers were dangerous men, drunken and lawless. In 1800, protesting against redundancies, they marched on the flour mills of Ulverston and looted them. Pursued by the militia,

74

they retreated into the holes of the mountainside. Right up to the First World War, quarrymen lived rough on the hill through the working week, sending messages down to their wives in Borrowdale by carrier pigeon.

Moses Rigg himself—wadd smuggler, slate miner, or even whisky distiller—is more mystery than actual man, with legends from several different centuries attached. He was, for certain, a lover of Great Gable. And his path around it, with its crag view above and its Ennerdale view outwards, is convenient and secret, supposing you have a pocketful of stolen graphite or a pony loaded with whisky. And even if you're totally legit, it still remains one of the mountain's special pleasures.

ROUTE 9 From Honister, over Grey Knotts and Green Gable

Start:	Honister Hause
Distance to summit:	4km (2½miles)
Total ascent:	650m (2,200ft)
Terrain:	Clear paths, becoming steep and rugged after Windy Gap.

How good? Interesting and varied, with less ascent than other routes.

A steep pitched path (signed 'Grey Knotts') climbs from behind the quarry buildings to a stile high on Grey Knotts. Once across the fence, the path turns left alongside it. A further stile on the left gives access to Grey Knotts' rocky little summit. The fence leads on, south across Brandreth to a wide col with small peat-tarns, Gillercomb Head.

A wide path runs up, with drops on the left into Gillercomb, to reach Green Gable's summit. An eroded path zigzags down into Windy Gap, then heads straight uphill on scree ledges separated by low rock walls, to the summit plateau. Here the path becomes unclear on the stony ground, but is marked by cairns, west then south-west to the summit rock knoll.

ROUTE 9A Climbers' traverse under Gable Crag

How good? A charming little path, now almost unused.

From Windy Gap, the Climbers' Traverse contours out right, then slants down along the foot of the crags. It passes below Easy Gully (scree, with a boulder in the middle), rounds the lowest point of Gable Crag, and makes a gently rising traverse along the crag foot, at once crossing below the next gully. At the far corner of the crag, contour forward to join Gable's steep south-west spur, about 100m above the platform on it where Moses Trod arrives.

In reverse: Leave the south-west spur level with the near-bottom corner of Gable Crag, on a very small contouring path between two boulders with cairns. Follow it along the foot of the crag all the way.

9 Grave Gable

Upon this rock are set the names of men—our brothers, and our comrades upon these cliffs—who held, with us, that there is no freedom of the soil where the spirit of man is in bondage; and who surrendered their part in that fellowship of hill and wind and sunshine, that the freedom of this land, the freedom of the spirit, should endure.

Geoffrey Winthrop Young, Gable summit, 1924

It's usually said that the Fell and Rock Climbing Club's war memorial is sited at the top of Great Gable. This isn't quite correct. The Fell and Rock Club's war memorial *is* Great Gable, together with the surrounding fells including Lingmell and Kirk Fell. Club members purchased the mountains, at the same time as Lord Leconfield was buying the summit of Scafell Pike. The combined ground was then presented to the National Trust as a monument for all time. At 3,210ft high, and nearly five square miles, this must be the world's largest war memorial.

The bronze relief map of the purchased fells was

designed and cast by club members, and set in place during the summer of 1924.

Among those heading up out of Warnscale Bottom on 8th June 1924 was a club member who had driven ambulances on the Isonzo front: a battlefield where half a million died, but which is now largely forgotten, along the Soca (formerly Isonzo) river in the Julian Alps of what is now Slovenia but was then the Italian/Austrian border. It was a campaign at least as futile as the trenches of Flanders. The Austrian positions on Krn and Monte San Gabriele were carved into solid rock, and the Italians seem to have attacked them mainly to maintain status with respect to their stronger allies France and Britain. But unlike Flanders, the Isonzo (or Piave) Campaign was fought among mountains of great loveliness, across the green waters of a winding limestone river.

Geoffrey Winthrop Young had been, before the Great War, one of Britain's leading climbers: a companion of Mallory, the Everest climber. On a summer night in August 1917, during the fight for Monte San Gabriele, he drove his ambulance along a moonlit road on the gorge-side high above the Isonzo River. His vehicle was struck by shellfire, and he lost his left leg just below the knee. June

1924 saw him attempting, on the wooden leg he'd designed himself, his first serious hill walk. The day was unpromising: wind, driving rain, and cloud completely hid the upper hill. He was still unused to the new leg, and had not learnt, as he did later, to ignore as illusory all feelings of exhaustion for at least the first four hours. It did not lift his spirits to be passing painfully across ground which he had in earlier years hared across. 'Hared' quite literally—he was the co-inventor of the game of the Trevelyan Hunt described in Chapter 10.

At Windy Gap the weather was no better, and it seemed he would not make the summit in time. But then he heard footsteps on the scree: footsteps that surrounded him on all sides. And as the wind blew gaps in the cloud, he became aware of silent walkers climbing alongside and around his party, approaching the summit out of Borrowdale, and Ennerdale, as well as on his own path. In silence, apart from the scrape of nailed boots on rock, the climbers and walkers gathered on the summit. The bugle sounded, echoing off the unseen mountains all around; and as its notes died, the cloud opened enough to let a pale shaft of sunlight break through to the summit and the newly placed bronze plaque. And by a quirk of the atmosphere, mist-lost walkers on Green Gable heard Winthrop Young's tribute, coming down 'trumpet-like' across Windy Gap.

Those words stress the double aim of the memorial: not just to mark the twenty names of the fallen climbers, but also to preserve for all time their hills for us, the walkers and climbers of later ages.

By this ceremony we consecrate a twofold remembrance; in token that these men gave their mortality of manhood for a redemption of earthly freedom, this rock stands, a witness, perishable also in the onset of time, that this realm of mountain earth is, in their honour, free …

By this symbol we affirm a twofold trust: that which hills only can give their children, the disciplining of strength in freedom, the freeing of the spirit through generous service, these free hills shall give again, and for all time.

Among the names on the tablet, S F Jeffcoat is the eponym of Jeffcoat's Ledge on Scafell Crag. H L Slingsby is not, however, Cecil Slingsby, the pioneering climber commemorated by Slingsby's Chimney on Scafell Crag, but his son Laurence. Years before, Winthrop Young had climbed Gable by its icy Ennerdale face with both Slingsbys, and brought young

Laurence down to Wasdale sitting on his shoulders. But the most notable of the names from a climbing point of view, and another of Young's former companions, is S W Herford.

Siegfried Herford created routes on Kern Knotts crag, and the back of the Napes Needle. But he will always be most famous as the climber of Central Buttress, the 140m face at the centre of Scafell Crag. It was a climb 'of uncommon daring' that pushed standards forward by about twenty years and that remained a classic test-piece at Hard Very Severe standard even with nylon ropes and modern levels of protection. Winthrop Young first met Herford standing on the summit of Tryfan, at sunset: 'a sturdy and tattered figure with a shock of strong flaxen hair'. Described as a promising physicist 'but a poet at heart', the achiever of Central Buttress was not seen by the British Army as officer material and died in the trenches with the rank of private. One of his climbing companions encountered his ghost at Hollow Stones, below his great climb, on what turned out to have been the same day that he died. On Gable, the likeliest spot to meet the handsome but old-fashioned youth possibly not of this world will be on the Screes Path below another of his climbs, Kern Knotts West Buttress.

The Fell and Rock Climbing Club's memorial plaque at Gable's summit

To help you recognise him, Herford's hill dress was tweed jacket and white pullover, puttees and nailed boots.

Nowadays, walkers and climbers gather at the summit on Remembrance Day, the first Sunday after 11th November. The weather usually matches that of the inauguration, but November can also give days of cold, clear sunshine. A fairly early start is needed to reach the summit for the two-minute silence at 11 o'clock; and parking may be a problem, especially at Honister. The bright nylon jackets of several hundred walkers contrast with the original ceremony, where the only touch of colour was the battle flag flown at Jutland by HMS Barham, and used for unveiling the plaque. The names written there are only now familiar from the first-ascents section of rock-climbing guides. But Gable remains a place to consider the freedom of the hills, and the sacrifice and futility of war.

Geoffrey Winthrop Young's account of the dedication of the Gable Memorial, and of his gradual return to the mountains as a one-legged climber, are in *Mountains with a Difference* (Eyre & Spottiswoode, 1951; out of print). The full text of his tribute is on the Fell and Rock Climbing Club's website (www. frcc.co.uk).

ROUTE 10 Gillercomb

Start: Seathwaite, Borrowdale

Distance to summit: 4km (2½ miles)

Total ascent: 850m (2,800ft)

Terrain: Path, rather steep to start with but well-built.

How good? A route of great charm, first alongside the waterfalls and then into the hidden valley above.

Follow the road-end into Seathwaite farm, and (just before the café) turn right through an arch to a wide path. This runs across the valley to a footbridge over the infant River Derwent. Keep straight ahead, up a steep stepped path to the left of Sour Milk Gill. The path is well-engineered, but has some slightly rocky sections.

Quite suddenly, you find yourself at the top of the waterfalls on the level, grassy floor of Gillercomb. The path heads up the left side of the hanging valley, then zigzags up its steeper headwall to the grassy neck between Base Brown and Green Gable. It turns right, and reaches Green Gable's gentle north ridge at a fairly large cairn. (In descent in mist, it's easy to miss this path-turn and continue on a smaller path towards Brandreth.)

The path runs up left, with cairns, to Green Gable summit. It joins Route 9 to zigzag down into Windy Gap where you can divert to the Gable Crag traverse (Route 9A) or keep straight ahead up Great Gable (Route 9).

ROUTE 10A Sour Milk Gill
300m/1,000ft of scrambling Grade 1 or 2

How good? A splendid and rather popular scramble, with lots of good rock, easy escape at any point, scenic situations and, from the upper part, good views as well. The route chosen will depend on water levels and on the ambition of the scrambler.

Cross the valley floor and enter the stream bed. From the footbridge it's boulder-scrambling below gloomy trees until the stream splits, with the left-hand (south) branch being rockier and more interesting. After they rejoin, the scrambling becomes more continuous. This lower part of the scramble is under trees; here the rocks under the stream are clean but those alongside it are slippery with brown algae, while bare rock on the hillside on the right gives very easy alternatives.

A small waterfall (still inside the wood) can be climbed on dry rock on its right, or by a slimed rib midstream, where waterwashed footholds and incut handholds make an easier way than it looks. The gill emerges from the trees to a high, splashy, wide waterfall, this fall being visible from the valley below. Here, as on most of this upper ground, there are hard routes in or close to the stream, and easy rock slabs and grass on the hillside on the right, but the best route is between these two, following or just below the gill rim.

A short steep wall is overlapped by the slats of a new fence. At the next substantial fall, a seasonal stream-line to the left of the main flow gives a splashy climb on clean footholds with good handholds.

The final fall is most romantic, with a rock outjut-ment splitting its top. A dry gully to the right of the fall is the obvious way out, and it can be embellished by climbing to the left into the gap behind a pin-nacle, right alongside the falling water. Then traverse back right, to rejoin the dry gully. At its top you emerge to the moor beside the now gentle stream at the entrance to Gillercomb.

ROUTE 10B North-east ridge of Base Brown

How good? A demanding but rewarding ridge ascent.

Follow Route 10 or 10A to the top of Sour Milk Gill, then turn left and confront the ridge of Base Brown. It rises to a crag that blocks the ridge line.

Go up grass and boulders, to pass a huge slabby boulder. Pass left above it, finding a trace of path, which gets clearer as you work up to the foot of the confronting crag. Here the path contours out left for 50 metres, passing below a rowan tree, quite exposed, then turns sharply up right. The path is clear, now to the left of the most broken ground. It slants up grass between small outcrops, then fades before reaching the crest. A few metres up the crest on the right is a large perched boulder, the Hanging Stone, that was visible from below the crag. (Care in descent: the path is not easy to find from the top—20 metres below the Hanging Stone bear off right.)

Continue easily up the ridge crest, crossing a level section at 550m altitude. A small path forms to pass the cairned summit. Cross the grassy neck towards Green Gable; at the neck's lowest point, rejoin the large path (Route 10) coming up out of Gillercomb.

10 Trevelyan Hunt

And the thrill of the kill

Did you never hear of the 'Lake Hunt' of past days?—when there were no motor coaches, and the day's letters jogged up in a pony cart, something after twelve, and there were no hot-baths there, nor cold baths either, but the same Elysian pool under the big rock, where there is a foot-bridge today and curious eyes? In those great days of old, men ran upon the fells, chasing fleet long-distance champions and high hopes of dinner in the evening.

H H Symonds, *Walking in the Lake District*, 1933

What is fun for? Ignoring certain subtleties, fun is the chemical on-button: it's the organism telling itself to do this thing again. A properly evolved organism ought, accordingly, to tell itself to do just those things that enhance its survival into later generations, while avoiding the ones that lead to a quick and messy death.

This theory makes it difficult to explain the enjoyable aspects of rock climbing, or rock music, or simple slobbing about on the sofa eating unhealthy snacks. It identifies such cultural acts as watching football matches, or reading this book, as pointless and so presumably pretty boring. For what's fun is what's good for you and for your present or future offspring.

Thus there are three forms of fun that are truly fundamental. Two of them are food and flirtation. The third form of fun is the hunt.

Our day started from a crouching position at the break of the slope above Gillercomb. Gillercomb is good; a hidden bit of territory that rival humans may not have found out about, enclosed in crags and sheltered under the scree wall of Base Brown. The viewpoint was a good one, between two outcrops but with clear sight-lines along the wide grass floor of the valley. Just one problem: no prey. No unsuspecting elk, no mammoth browsing its way towards a point where its retreat would be over the Sour Milk water-fall. Not so much as a marmot or a bunny.

And so we worked around by Windy Gap to the Ennerdale face of Gable. And below us we saw what we were after. Not the fellwalkers on Haystacks: those we treated as invisible. But below us, on the pathless slope above the stream, a member of a tasty prey species was heading cautiously down-valley. We crouched and, communicating by hand gestures, spread ourselves along Moses Trod until we covered 400 metres of fell above our quarry.

Two minutes later, that quarry passed below one of the glaciated outcrops. It was the moment. Unobserved, we rose from the rushes and charged downhill. Two of us split off to come on our victim from behind. The rest of us spread out ahead and dropped. A few seconds later, the prey appeared directly below, moving now at a run and glancing anxiously backwards.

We let our victim run under us for a little longer, then rose again from cover and ran. Directly below me now, it turned downhill. But I was fresh, and in my Walsh fellrunning shoes. I lengthened my stride, and struck.

The party gathered around our kill where it lay in the peaty ground a few metres from the stream. Briefly and Britishly we congratulated each other. My own brain was flooding with atavistic chemicals. Teamwork had worked; and I myself had struck the quarry down. I felt for it, as it lay at my feet, a rush of love almost religious in its intensity. I sat down beside it and gave it a pat.

The quarry sat up, and removed the faded once-crimson sash. 'Very good,' it commented. 'Excellent. I never saw you up there at all.'

It had all been only a game. That game is known variously as the Trevelyan Hunt or the Trinity Hunt, depending on whether you're doing it in May or in June. Its two inventors were George Macaulay Trevelyan, the historian, and Geoffrey Winthrop Young, schoolteacher and mountaineer, who has already visited Great Gable in Chapter 9. Its playing field is Upper Ennerdale and Gable, with the wonderful hummocky ground of Haystacks and an occasional foray into the old quarries of Fleetwith Pike. Over the century of the game, the red sashes have been reinforced and patched. The rules—basically the playground game of catch—have remained much the same.

Any game needs rules. Technically, these ones don't work very well: nothing in them prevents the hare from lurking all day among the Sitka spruce trees boringly uncaught. But in practice they're even better than football for arousing the ancient hormones.

We are an animal that wants to eat, to have sex, and to get together in a group to chase down an elk. Or else to stand at Westmorland Cairn surveying the terrain, find an unexpected way down between the ridges, then leap out suddenly and grab an elk all on our own. It's what fellwalking is for. Except that up the Breast Path in a queue of rucksacked strangers isn't actually a very exciting simulation. For more authentic fake-hunting you need to be working across the untrodden scree face of Haystacks, with two pursuers behind, and a man with binoculars directing them from down beside the Black Sail hostel.

I couldn't break uphill; they were already slightly above me. There was no point in heading down, towards the man who could move across smooth grass to intercept. I just had to keep contouring and try to pull away from them. I tried to pull away; but they kept up.

And then I came upon a little strip of scree between two heathery ribs. Most scree in Lakeland has been shifted to slope's foot by the million-footed fellwalker. But nobody walks the broken slope of Haystacks. Three seconds later I was 20 metres down the slope.

Where they last see you, their minds continue the line. Assuming myself out of sight, I turned back uphill beyond the rock rib, grabbing heather stalks to regain ten of the metres I'd lost, and snuggled down into the heather. I'd been lucky. They must have been unsighted, and not even seen my scree descent. And the man with the glasses down below had presumably scanned on across the slope for my reappearance, scanned back, and found he'd forgotten where I'd last been. By the time they'd realised that I was no longer in front, they'd already moved on 100 metres. I lay still, enjoying the scent of the damp heather and the safety.

They knew I was somewhere, and that I couldn't move without being seen from below. They quickly realised that they'd passed me. And ten minutes later, a man broke the skyline 20 metres away and his eyes met mine.

But 20 metres was enough. They'd been searching in very rough country and I'd been having a rest. Behind by 20 metres they were, and at 20 metres I could hold them, while at the same time slipping some upwards into my contouring. Ten minutes later, and I entered the cloud. I put in a couple of zigzags to complete their confusion, leant against a rock in the welcome drizzly greyness, and enjoyed a sandwich. Then I wandered gently up towards Haystacks' knolly plateau.

Two plateau walkers loomed out of the mist:

walkers who stopped, registered my soaking-wet red sash, and started running urgently towards me. I was tired and they were fresh. But I remembered the fell shoes on my feet; and headed back over the edge, and down a slope of steep and slippery grass. To hear, from behind, the very welcome words: 'Oh, bugger!'

Evolution shaped our brains during a million years of Stone Age lifestyle. In such a lifestyle, an intimate knowledge of the paths around Great Gable might lead to intimacy of a more productive sort, as we sneak over for some reproductive fun among the women of Ennerdale. And when the men of Ennerdale come back to burn our huts and take over our territory, we can retreat into Hell Gate, hide our babies, and roll down boulders.

Fellwalking isn't simply what we do because we see the other two million already at it. It's more than a convenient way of flooding our blood with opiates and serotonin without risking arrest or dirty needles. Fellwalking is necessary; so that as soon as we stopped doing it in daily life we had to invent it as a game. Standing on Great Gable naming every summit in sight: this may be boring, but it's a survival skill. And at day's end, a million years of history is narrowing our eyes and crouching our limbs as we drop for the last time into the head of Gillercomb. At the sight of the prey, lonely on the wide grassland, go-for-it chemicals flood into our legs and override the tiredness, don't-think-about-it enzymes incite our minds to a plunge through the woods and boulders on the unpathed side of Sour Milk Gill. It's the most natural thing in the world to leap out of the plantation, chase the quarry into the River Derwent, and leap in after. A few muscle strains and scratches are nothing when the prize is 50 kilos of fresh meat, with all that it implies in small-group prestige, sexual opportunity, and status-gain in the queue for the cooling secondhand bathwater at Seatoller. In that final encounter, sadly, I was not the valiant pursuer but the prey. You can't win them all.

ROUTE 11 Aaron Slack

Start:	Seathwaite, Borrowdale
Distance to summit:	4½km (2½ miles)
Total ascent:	770m (2,600ft)
Terrain:	Path, gentle at first, becoming steep and rough.

How good? Harsh and not particularly rewarding, with comparatively poor views. More sheltered than other routes.

> *If I could know who Aaron was*
> *Who put down all that slack,*
> *I'd throw him into Styhead tarn*
> *And hope to break his back.*
>
> quoted in H H Symonds,
> *Walking in the Lake District*, 1933
> (slack = small lumps, as in 'nutty slack'
> in your coal hole long ago)

From Seathwaite, take the wide path south, to the left of the River Derwent. Turn right across Stockley Bridge and slant up west around Greenhow Knott to meet Styhead Gill. After 800 metres the path crosses at a footbridge and turns upstream again.

Immediately before reaching Styhead Tarn, the path crosses a small stream at a big cairn. Turn uphill straight afterwards, on the Aaron Slack path, which is initially unclear, to the left of the stream. As the side walls rise on either side, the path crosses the stream, becoming stony and all too obvious up to Windy Gap. Here turn left, on a path that crosses scree, bare rock and boulderfield to the summit.

ROUTE 11A Taylorgill Force

How good? A tougher and much less busy route, past a fine waterfall.

At Seathwaite turn right under an arch, to cross the River Derwent by a footbridge, and turn left on a rough path to the right (west) of the stream. It runs next to the stream, then slants up right, entering a woodland regeneration area at a kissing gate and leaving it at a ladder stile at the top of a felled plantation. Not particularly clear, it slants up to pass along the base of crags to a gate just round the corner (NY231111) for a brief scramble to reach the top of Taylorgill Force.

The well-situated gate below Taylorgill

Continue to the right of the beck to join the main path (see Route 11 above) at its footbridge.

11 Pharmacology of fellwalking

Going again and again up Great Gable is not something you actually choose to do. You just find you need more and more of Gable to get the same effect. On days that don't have Gable in them, you're getting twitchy and irritable. Moses Trod and Aaron Slack are interfering with your relationships with actual human beings. You're neglecting your working life, your sex life, and even your lunch, for the sake of the Sphinx Ridge.

You are not to be blamed for this. It's not a bad habit, or a depravity in the will, and no amount of guilt will get you over it. Great Gable is an illness. You're not vicious: you're the victim of an addiction.

It's true that, at the foot of the sudden steep path of Aaron Slack, you don't see the fellwalkers rolling up their Gore-Tex sleeves and shoving in a needleful of heroin. But this is simply because they've found a more convenient and cheaper way. For them, simply walking up the Sty Head path has done the trick. They're getting high on Great Gable, and, at the same time, high on a chemical substance called endorphin.

Endorphin works something like this. As the walker starts to perform strenuous exertions with the legs and feet, a message comes up from the muscles: 'Don't do this! You're burning up calories, and risking injury to our stringy bits. Why not drive back to the B&B and watch an Alfred Wainwright video?'

We all know those 'don't-do-this' messages, aimed at stopping us burning away the last of the glycogen fuel from that bowl of muesli we hunted down and gathered for our breakfast. However, if we obeyed those messages all the time, we'd never get any more muesli. (Well, we wouldn't if muesli really was something we had to track down for hours across the face of Gable.) If we persist in exerting our feet upwards, presumably we're fleeing a persistent lion or tiger below; or maybe we've sighted a flirtatious young person or a tasty elk ahead.

Nature isn't always straightforward. Instead of just switching off the don't-do-this, nature has provided an override. The chemicals called endorphins are a powerful 'do-do-this' signal. They dull the perception of pain, and send us up surges of niceness. They squirt out of your pituitary gland, which is in your brain, but it's not a part of your brain and it doesn't think. It's a chemical regulator, operating at a vegetable level of intelligence. It simply checks for certain chemicals in your bloodstream or sap, and responds by squirting in chemicals of its own. And incidentally, you didn't have to come all the way up here to get it. Research has shown that for a surge of endorphin it's enough for someone just to give you a good, sound, spanking.

But spanking's not your scene. So set off up the path from Seathwaite. For the first few steps, the exciting sights ahead draw you forward. But then the legs kick in with their messages of pain. You ignore them, and the pain gets slightly worse. 'Turn back, turn back,' say the legs: 'or better still, stop!' Between your lips emerge groans, calculated to make your companions feel sorry for you and slow down. But they don't, despite your reproachful glances directed at their vanishing backs. However, as you continue to pace valiantly forward, the endorphin message comes flooding down the bloodstream. It wipes out the pain sensations, and induces in the head a happy hillwalkers' glow. 'I'm okay now,' you say, 'I've got my second wind.'

And so, in a comfortable balance of 'don't-do' leg messages and 'do-do' endorphin in the head, you walk the two miles up to Sty Head. But now comes the sprawling cairn, and the small ford, and it's time to turn sharply to the right and uphill on Aaron's Slack. The pain messages abruptly increase. About 30 metres up Aaron's Slack you stop and look back and see Styhead Tarn spread out a very short distance below. And you think: 'If it hurts this much already, how am I ever going to get up to the top?'

But nobody else is going to do it for you, so you turn around and head uphill. And, oddly, another 30 metres up you stop thinking about how little you've done. The nice chemicals have surged up to overcome the new level of nastiness; and so you walk on, examining the small stones in the path, or the V-shaped wedge of Wasdale over the pass, or thinking about the pre-payment plan on your mobile phone.

Now, if you stop on the way up, the pain goes away at once; but the pleasant pituitary chemicals also slowly peter out. When you move on up, you've got the agony again, but without the endorphin. Accordingly, wise old birds go uphill slow and steady. In the same way, at a party, they'll trickle the alcohol in all evening, while the young folk are taking six quick whiskies, then going to the toilets to throw up.

So be temperate, and keep steady but slow: and after a while emerge at Windy Gap.

Here, a new chemical comes into the buzzing bloodstream. Rocks have to be clambered over, and, unless you're completely used to this sort of thing, a thrill of danger zips out of a small gland just on top of your liver, plunges its sharp needle into your artery, and injects you with adrenalin.

Normally the body runs at a comfortable rate, maximising the miles per gallon and not putting too much wear on the clutch. Adrenalin shoots all the systems into overdrive. The heart speeds up: the stomach shuts down and diverts its bloodstream to the muscles. The eyes open extra-wide, the face takes on a terrible grimace in case there's an enemy nearby needing intimidation. Sweat leaps from the pores as the body's cooling system prepares for hot action. The skin pales as the blood retreats inwards: this is to minimise spillage in the event of any limbs being torn off in the coming encounter. The pain sensors are told to shut down for a while and stop complaining.

For those in offices, adrenalin means seething but stifled urges to shout rude words at the computer; and this is bad for you. But on the hill, adrenalin means I'm going to bash my way up this hill and leap across the chasm. It means I'm bigger and braver than it is and it's not going to stop me. Adrenalin makes hare-person and hunter-person run full tilt down Aaron Slack, fall head-first, and—assuming legs aren't actually broken—roll straight to feet and keep on running. And the thing about adrenalin is that it feels just great at the time, and it also feels great afterwards—assuming you didn't actually break any of those legs.

And then you stop at the summit; and lay the legs on the ground before you. But the endorphin keeps on surging out of your pituitary gland. And what you're looking at is seen through a pleasant hormonal haze. Never mind the Sublime in high landscape; it's endorphin surge and adrenalin afterglow that tints the view across Haystacks and that distant glimpse of Crummock Water.

But after half an hour, the pleasant chemicals die down, and you get a bit chilly as well, and you stand up and start to walk downhill. Oh dear! The delicate downhill work doesn't let you stride manfully (or womanfully) to re-induce the endorphin effect. Your toes are sore. And it's an awful long way to Honister...

The juice of the poppy contains a chemical that, by a fluke of pharmacology, mimics those natural hormones called endorphin—the word 'endorphin' just means internal opium. You can buy the poppy stuff at Piccadilly Circus and shove it in your arm. Or you can be a bit more natural, and generate your own inside your pituitary gland. At the same time, you're getting high on another hormone called serotonin— the commercial, synthetic version is known as LSD. Many fellrunners are well aware of the chemical nature of their addiction. Run hard for several hours: up Great Gable, say, in the Borrowdale Race. Then leap like a peculiarly ugly sort of chamois down the little rock steps and scree, concentration fierce, and maybe sneakily overtake someone in an Ambleside vest who's not quite so good at it. Then hands on knees and shove up the zigzag scree to Green Gable. But then comes the grassy slope beyond, just at the angle for flying at maximum stride with air resistance balancing gravity. The anguish-effort level drops to not much more than that of a normal hill walk, while the grossly elevated endorphin blows your head off. Some psychologists don't believe in 'runner's high'—but that was me running down Green Gable, and I know. It strongly recalls degenerate days of the 1960s when hair was long and limbs were thin. Once you've paid for the petrol and the special shoes, the running experience is possibly more expensive than the Mexican hemp ever was. It's equally bad for the health but in completely different ways. The surroundings lack Pink Floyd music, and posters by Alphonse Mucha; but grey rain flying past the face at 20mph also has a bit of psychedelic thrill.

This level of addiction carries the usual punishment. Runners deprived of their fix become edgy and irritable. Fortunately, a good groin strain will usually induce a six-month period of compulsory withdrawal. This lets you stand back, wonder whether that hideous aluminium statuette (3rd Veteran Blisco Dash) is really recompense for only ever drinking beer on Sundays, and decide to rejoin that portion of the human race whose toenails are not black but normal pink in colour.

Meanwhile, the rest of us are down at Wasdale Head, augmenting the Great Gable afterglow with judicious draughts of the Great Gable ale. Opiates and a hint of LSD; alcohol and adrenalin: it's just one big druggy day.

ROUTE 12 The Screes Path

Start: Sty Head

Finish: Beck Head

Distance: 2km (1¼ miles)

Terrain: The path is narrow and quite exposed, with a little scrambling here and there (perhaps just Grade 1 on the descent to Little Hell Gate).

How good? The best path on Great Gable, but not a path *up* Great Gable at all!

This narrow and in places awkward path runs above and across the screes overlooking Wasdale. It passes below the Great Napes and White Napes Buttresses and the two Hell Gates, giving access to all these.

Reach Sty Head from Borrowdale by Route 11 or (better) 11A, then continue past Styhead Tarn to the stretcher box at the pass. From Wasdale, use Route 3 or (better) 3A.

The stretcher box is labelled 'Stretcher Box' in large letters. According to Wasdale Mountain Rescue legend, a walker did once try it as a comfortable resting spot out of the rain. But at that time the box was self-latching, and the walker accordingly became the only one ever to be rescued from inside the rescue box.

The stretcher box marks a major path crossroads. Downhill north-east, the wide path runs past Styhead Tarn to Borrowdale. Downhill the other way, the wide path slants down the right-hand side of Spouthead Gill's valley, crossing the flank of Gable towards Wasdale. At right-angles to these, a path runs east, through the lowest point of the saddle, towards Sprinkling Tarn and the Corridor Route up Scafell Pike. Opposite that, the pitched Breast Path runs north-west, directly up Great Gable.

Between the Breast Path and the Wasdale Path, a less distinct path slants uphill west-north-west, becoming invisible across a grassy patch and reforming beyond, where it contours across the face of Gable. With the small but steep Kern Knotts crag ahead, a slightly out-of-balance move leads on to a rock ledge. Descend from the ledge to pass through the boulders below Kern Knotts, losing height as you do so, to find a clear path beyond.

This climbs again to pass below a small square cave with a spring inside it. Scramble up, 10 metres left of the cave, to join the upper of two paths slanting across the scree beyond (or contour below the cave to join the lower path). Across the scree, you reach a spur of grass and broken rocks. (The lower path zigzags up this spur to rejoin.) Contour around the broken ground, on a small and slightly exposed path, to reach the screes of Great Hell Gate, with the Great Napes towering above on the far side.

Cross the scree, on a path slithered away in places, to the broken ground beyond. Pass below the foot of a small steep rock wall, and up broken ground briefly: the Napes Needle is visible ahead and above. The path contours across a narrow scree-run (for Route 16, Great Hell Gate, turn up the left edge of this scree). The small path keeps contouring, about 50m below the base of the Needle. Cross the scree-run of Needle Gully. Now the Cat Rock (which doubles as the Sphinx) is skylined ahead and above. Cross another narrow scree running down from the near side of the Sphinx, then pass below the Sphinx. Now the path descends a rock groove for about 20m—slightly awkward and exposed at the top, with another near-Grade 1 move at the very foot, where you emerge on the screes of Little Hell Gate. The path contours across the scree to the broken ground of the White Napes opposite.

Things now get easier. At the corner of the slope, small cairns mark the path as it contours across the wide screes of Gable's west face. Stay on the same level, ignoring nasty descending paths, to reach the broad col of Beck Head.

Ascend Gable's steep north-west spur, or continue on the Gable Crag path (Route 9A, reversed).

In reverse: The start of the path is awkward to find, particularly in mist. From the eastern edge of the Beck Head col, find the cairned path descending south, towards Wasdale. Go down this for 20 metres, then contour out left, looking for a few small cairns. Once on the screes, the path becomes clearly defined.

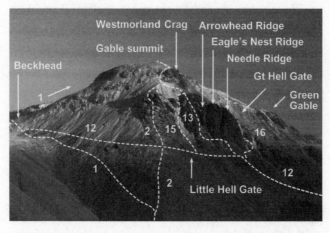

Routes 12–16 on the Great Napes

12 In Search of the Sublime

Insensate Seathwaite, what art thou but an assemblage of rocks, stones, clods, clumps and trees? Our imagination it was that vivified thee with beauty—till thou becamest symbolical of all spiritual essences, embodied poetry of a paradisiacal state of being.

Christopher North (real name Professor John Wilson), *Letters from the Lakes*, 1819

The passion caused by the great and sublime in nature, where these causes operate most powerfully, is Astonishment; and astonishment is that state of the soul, in which all its motions are suspended, with some degree of horror.

Burke, *Philosophical Enquiry*, Section I

In 1769 the poet Thomas Gray had a frightening time in Borrowdale: 'the rocks at the top deep-cloven perpendicularly by the rains, hanging loose and leaning forwards ... The road on both sides is strewed with piles of the fragments, strangely thrown across each other, and of dreadful bulk.' Anxious about avalanches and landslides, he only got as far as Grange: 'All further access is here barred to prying mortals.'

It's customary to mock Thomas Gray for being such a wimp. Gray certainly wasn't brave; but at the same time he was a practitioner of an art now largely lost: the discriminating appreciation of natural landscape. The (largely imaginary) terrors of the Jaws of Borrowdale were an important part of his technique. We could compare him with a wine-drinker of today, going on about the rich fruit and the hint of strawberry and the sharp splinter of tannin inserted into the nose. If the fellow really wanted strawberries he could go in the garden and pick some, and save the £25 for the St Emilion. His strawberries aren't the pink and squishy ones of the real world, but a sensory signpost. He wants to point our tongues in a particular direction, with the aim of extracting 25 quid's worth of pleasure out of our plonk. In the same way, Gray's description, while guiding the feet between the Jaws of Borrowdale, was also guiding the mind towards a specific experience—one known as the Sublime.

The cult of Picturesque Beauty came into being when wealthy young men returned from the Grand Tour of Europe with the paintings of Claude Lorrain,

Nicolas Poussin and Salvator Rosa glowing in their memories or, if they really were wealthy, in their suitcases. They then superimposed these pictures on their own estates (expensively but ably assisted by Lancelot 'Capability' Brown) and on the scenery of England.

The handbook of this particular training regime for eyeball and mind was *Observations, relative chiefly to Picturesque Beauty*, by William Gilpin, whose main visit to Lakeland was in 1772. But for 'Picturesque Beauty for Dummies' we can turn to Jane Austen. Jane Austen admired Gilpin, but at the same time was not unaware of the absurdity of his project. Here, in *Northanger Abbey*, seventeen-year old Catherine Morland is receiving instruction in the art of landscape appreciation. The scene is, even today, a lovely viewpoint at the southern edge of Bath:

> *It seemed as if a good view were no longer to be taken from the top of a high hill, and that a clear blue sky was no longer a proof of a fine day. She was heartily ashamed of her ignorance ... a lecture on the picturesque immediately followed, in which Mr Tilney's instructions were so clear that she soon began to see beauty in every thing admired by him. He talked of fore-grounds, distances, and second distances—side-screens and*

Force of the imagination? Taylorgill in 1832, by Thomas Allom

*perspectives—lights and shades; and Catherine
was so hopeful a scholar, that when they gained
the top of Beechen Cliff, she voluntarily rejected
the whole city of Bath, as unworthy to make part
of a landscape.*

Beauty—whether findable at Bath or not—was
not the highest form of landscape experience. Better than beauty, and in some respects its opposite,
was the Sublime. The starkness and simplicity of the
Scottish landscape, Gilpin explains, which 'no doubt
injures the beauty, is at the same time the source of
sublimity.' The Lake Country has both beauty and
sublimity:

*Sometimes one prevails: sometimes the other: and
sometimes we are struck with the united force of
both. Ideas of simple grandeur were generally suggested between Keswick, and Ambleside; and of
beauty chiefly between Ambleside, and Kendal.*

The concept of the Sublime goes back to the
ancient Greeks, where it was applied to the sort of
rhetoric that provokes strong feelings and over-
rides common sense. But for an eighteenth-century
account of it, we have the ambitious young writer
and politician, Edmund Burke, writing on what had
become the hot topic of 1757. Beauty, in Burke's

account, suggests the direct pleasures of our ordinary instincts. The soft, the curved and the cosy are beautiful: a small farm in a fertile country, a sexy person with no clothes on. The Sublime is borne upon the much stronger sensations associated with self-preservation: astonishment, awe, reverence, terror. Beauty suggests that something pleasant (a rest by a brook, a naked lady) is going to happen to me. The Sublime, contrariwise, suggests something nasty (an avalanche, a lion) that is *not* going to happen to me. And something scary that actually *is* going to happen suggests neither the Beautiful nor the Sublime, but rather that I should run away very quickly.

As suggested by both Gilpin and Gray, I started my search for the Sublime at the Keswick end of the Lakes. Borrowdale's Sour Milk Gill was showing plenty of water and a bit of ice at the side. Cataracts appeal, says Burke, because of their Power; this being a prime attribute of the Sublime. Power can be kindly and helpful or power can do harm: but which of the two do you actually expect from King George II or the Department of Social Security? The waterfall attracts because, although you're not actually going to, you could fall in and get swept away and arrive as a protein pinkness in Seathwaite's water supply.

The Hanging Stone on the north ridge of Base Brown is straight out of the landscape handbook. I'm not expecting it to fall (Wainwright drew it fifty years ago, so why should it topple today?) but I'm anxious anyway (there's a crag blocking the ridge above, and only fifteen minutes of daylight left for getting past it). But I'm now far enough above the valley to experience its Vastness and its Emptiness. Shadows gather along the valley floor, pierced by the scattered lights of Rosthwaite. And as I contour out left on the little path to avoid the crag, there's some of that shadowy emptiness almost directly below. (Vertical vastness is more impressive, says Burke, than vastness simply stretching away into the distance. He can't quite make up his mind whether vastness downwards is more, or less, sublime than vastness rising up.)

In his book *Status Anxiety*, the Sunday-supplement philosopher Alain de Botton argues that it's not being ugly and poor that makes us unhappy. Explorers and soldiers (and, of course, fellwalkers) put up with discomfort and deprivation worse than the most miserable members of our society, but still manage to enjoy themselves. What really gets people down is the way that other people are more adorable and rich than we are. And de Botton sees one remedy for this in mountain viewing. 'A fine remedy for anxieties about insignificance may be to travel—in reality or in works of art—through the gigantic spaces of the world.' When you and me are standing under Raven Crag, Gillercomb, we both look about the same size—very small. This makes me feel not quite so upset at the way you are 2cm taller than I am.

As an alternative therapy, de Botton suggests hanging about in graveyards. This makes us small and insignificant in time rather than in space: your gorgeous Porsche no longer matters once everybody's dead. Thomas Gray, who started this chapter by getting slightly scared at the sublimity of Borrowdale, became the all-time top graveyard frequenter with his poem 'Elegy Written in a Country Churchyard'.

The less you can see, the better the view. Dazzlement is one way to do sublimity: photos taken into the sun, perhaps with a bit of flare. But Obscurity and Darkness are easier. The half-seen inspires twice as much awe; Burke cites Milton's description of Death. ('Black he stood as night / And shook a deadly dart. What seemed his head / The likeness of a kingly crown had on.') The same point has been made by horror writer Stephen King. The monster is at his most frightening just before he leaps out from behind the shower curtain. And the generation that learnt to tremble deliciously at the 'wild forms of convulsed Nature' at Falcon Crag could go home to the fireside to read Mary Shelley's newly-published *Frankenstein*.

The boulders in front of my boot were getting harder to see, and darkness filled the hollows of Borrowdale. Moonlight ran across the summit of Base Brown, turning it into a rugged dome of uncertain size. New snow stood above the black crags of Great End. Across the valley, Glaramara swooped to its pointy knoll above Seathwaite, and the hills behind were drawn with a broad graphite pencil.

I found a hollow just below the wind. I unrolled my bag, and gazed up out of warm duck-down at patches of black sky with stars, and silvery cloud flapping across the moon like washing on a line. I put all my plastic bags back in the rucksack to silence their noise in the wind; I put my boots in as well, so they wouldn't freeze; and then I lay back for ten minutes, or it may have been an hour, enjoying the bigness of everything. After a time I stopped thinking at all.

It's just another of those mountain moments. It's not the moment when you step around the corner with the rope trailing behind, and see what the rock's got waiting for you. It's not the moment in running

Sublime scenes: Fleetwth Pike in 1853. Lithograph by Thomas Pyne

shoes in the rain and wind on the high ridge. It's not
the pause in the warm evening with friends beside

you and the valley waiting at the foot of the path. What it is, is the moment when the eyes open wide, and the mind closes down, and you breathe really slowly in the middle of the hills. Midwinter in the Mamores, with snowy ridges stretching 40 miles in all directions. The huge limestone hollows of the Picos de Europa. The ridge of Triglav, dropping 300m to a plain of rubble and twisted rock.

The boots didn't freeze overnight, but the water bottle did, so to find flowing water I went down to Sty Head, and had breakfast beside the tarn.

There were further aspects of the Sublime still to seek. An aesthetic tingle of Danger along the hard-frozen Screes Path, with lumps of water-ice decorating the ledges below Kern Knotts, and the big empty spaces of Wasdale below. 'Vacuity, Darkness, Solitude and Silence,' says Burke: 'with what a fire of imagination has Virgil amassed all these circumstances at the mouth of hell!' And quotes Dryden's translation from the Aeneid:

Obscure they went through dreary shades that led
Along the waste dominions of the dead.

Great Gable has its own Hell's Gate, where Effort and Difficulty are more than just a feeling. Misshapen pinnacles leer in from either side, and the stones slide in a widening fan all the way down to Lingmell Beck. Mud and gravel trickle off the wall of the White Napes. It's a place of endearing ugliness, with the atmosphere of a demolition site—which is, geologically speaking, exactly what it is.

After an hour of slithering in the screes I emerged to the grassy perch at the top of the Napes Ridges. Cloud blew around in the valley, opening in holes to show Wast Water running out to the grey sea. Pale sunlight brushed the walls of Westmorland Crag, and frost steamed off the ledges. Below, the towers and spikes of the Napes were black against orange scree and emerald moss.

The breaking of the craze

As is the way with crazes, Picturesque Beauty went out of fashion almost as quickly as it had come in. We've already seen Jane Austen mocking the jargon in the early 1800s. By the time of 'The Prelude' in 1805, Wordsworth was ashamed of his youthful enthusiasm for 'critic rules, and barren intermeddling subtleties', and envying the uninstructed eye of his sister Dorothy.

Even as the scary Sublime was going out as an idea, Lakeland was getting less scary in real life. Scenery seekers were finding their way to the summits and getting back down to the valleys still alive. The last wolf was shot (at Humphrey Head) in the 1790s.

This did not, however, mean that the landscape was to be looked at casually. Right at the end of his life, in his 'Disgusted of Rydal Mount' letter against the Windermere railway, Wordsworth argued that: 'rocks and mountains, torrents and wide spread waters, cannot, in their finer relations to the human mind, be comprehended without processes or opportunities of culture in some degree habitual.' (Letter to the *Morning Post*, 1844.)

In fact, Wordsworth took part in Gilpin's Picturesque programme: it was only Gilpin's book he rejected. His ideal was 'the spectator who has learned to observe and feel, chiefly from Nature herself'. That he was just such a spectator is shown by a new insight into the traditional categories of the beautiful and the sublime. Writing in his *Guide to the Lakes* (1810), about lakes:

> *The opposite sides of a profound vale may ascend as exact counterparts, like the billows of a troubled sea; and the impression be, from its very simplicity, more awful and sublime. Sublimity is the result of Nature's first great dealings with the*

124

*superficies of the earth; but the general tendency of
her subsequent operations is towards the produc-
tion of beauty; by a multiplicity of symmetrical
parts uniting in a consistent whole.*

Here he is observing, not categories of the imagination, but the real physical difference between glacial
and fluvial features: between the shapes carved (as we
now know) by water, and by ice. He also observed the
paradox of erratic boulders, carried on ridges by no
means we can see today; and in his youth, he had visited the Alps. How close he must have come, 35 years
before the geologists, to the sudden understanding of
Cumbria as a country once covered by glaciers.

Even at midnight, in midwinter, Lakeland today
is a pretty tame place; and somewhat small to be sublime. Familiarity breeds content but dissipates scari-
ness and awe. Gilpin and Wordsworth teach us to
look at Lakeland with close attention; standing still,
and in silence. That way we see more, and see more
intensely. But for the Sublime, we'll mostly need to
be somewhere bigger and more intimidating: the
Alps, the Picos, the Pyrenees. EasyJet and Ryanair
are today's conveyors of the eighteenth-century art of
landscape excess.

ROUTE 13 Napes Traverse and Sphinx Gully

Start:	Screes Path (Route 12) below Napes Needle
Total ascent:	200m scrambling height gain
Terrain:	Grade 1 scrambling on well-used clean rock, then indefinite but easier mountain scrambling.

How good? Reasonably easy scrambling on good rock in magnificent situations.

From Sty Head follow Route 12 below Kern Knotts and across Great Hell Gate screes. The path passes around the foot of a small buttress and goes up beyond it for 20 metres to a point below the bottom right-hand corner of the Great Napes. It turns left, contouring across a small scree run, to pass directly below Napes Needle (seen foreshortened from here).

Directly below the Needle, fork up right on a smaller path. This turns uphill to scramble easily straight up towards the Needle. A steep wall corner then has rather harder scrambling; to avoid this, turn left immediately below it, down a short groove into

Needle Gully. Ascend jammed boulders and scree to the foot of the Needle, and bear left up easy rock to the Dress Circle viewpoint of the famous photographs of the Needle.

Continue leftwards and up, on well-used rock, then traverse left across a slab. Having thus passed across the foot of Eagle's Nest Ridge, the well-marked way descends slightly into Eagle's Nest Gully. Traverse left into the slot between a tall block and the foot of Arrowhead Ridge. Pass through this gap.

Now an awkward out-of-balance move leads down into Arrowhead Gully. Various footholds are clearly trodden; the easiest way is to go up and left for a couple of metres, then swing down into the gully on large handholds.

From Arrowhead Gully's narrow scree strip, traverse onwards, on easier ground, towards the very conspicuous Sphinx Rock. (You could keep traversing, to pass behind the Sphinx, then descend a steep wall on good holds into Little Hell Gate, for continuations by Little Hell Gate, the White Napes, or the screes traverse to Beck Head.) Some 10 metres before the Sphinx, you reach the narrow scree strip of the ill-defined Sphinx Gully. Turn up this, on a trodden scrambling path.

Head straight up the small gully, with good hand-holds but scree on footholds. As the gully merges into the general face, the small path line continues upwards. More demanding and exposed scrambling lines are all around. A final steeper wall of clean rock offers an obvious challenge, but the path turns left along its foot, arriving on grassy slopes above the top of Little Hell Gate. Follow the path up to the grassy neck at the top of the Great Napes ridges.

Turn left along the grass ridge to meet the main mountain. Westmorland Crag rises above, and the path turns left along its foot. I've found Grade 1 scrambling up the left edge of the crag; but when I intended a repeat ascent for this route description, I was deterred by wet rock and thick cloud—so this option remains as an exploratory find-it-yourself. The path zigzags up scree to the left of Westmorland Crag. In clear viewing conditions, contour across the crag top to visit Westmorland Cairn; otherwise head directly uphill over stones to Gable summit.

13 Scrambled legs

Every healthy Englishman would be improved, morally and physically, by mountaineering.

> Owen Glynne Jones (who was not actually English but Welsh) in conversation, 1880s

People trifle with love. Now, I deny that love is a strong passion. Fear is the strong passion; it is with fear that you must trifle, if you wish to taste the intensest joys of living. Envy me—envy me, sir; I am a coward!

> Robert Louis Stevenson, 'The Suicide Club: Story of the Young Man with the Cream Tarts'

The brightest flowers grow on the borderland of Death.

> Frank Smythe, quoted in Hodge, *Enjoying the Lakes*, 1957

Sociologists have determined that we mountaineers like to create for ourselves a certain uncertainty. How much mystery we require depends on temperament:

Helm Crag, but do we take the sun cream? Or—Everest, and am I going to die in an avalanche? Between these two extremes is the question: can I, or can I not, get up through the Great Napes? Am I brave enough for this awkward step down into Arrowhead Gully?

There were obvious excuses not to. It was a raw, cloudy day. Our fingers on the handholds were chilled; our feet on the footholds were slightly slippery. On the other hand, those handholds are reassuringly big ones.

Behind us, the Napes Needle was an almost-visible spiky shadow within the grey. Below, the ground dropped in crag and scree for 20m, while the mist kindly concealed the further 500m of scree and crag below that. I swung round from the handholds, my foot found the rock, and I stepped down into the gully.

Ahead now, the Sphinx loomed dreamily among the raindrops. And our way was up, on small scree, and spiky handholds, and bits of trodden path that led to short rock steps and chimneys. Chunks of the Great Napes ridges drifted in and out of vision. The occasional rock-spike wobbled a little, but the way was reassuringly easy, and also reassuringly well-marked. At the same time, it was absorbing enough to stop us noticing the raindrops running down into our sleeves. We became aware of our wet elbows later on, as we emerged on the triangle of grass at the ridge top. Normally one of the magic viewpoints of all England, it was now a very small damp lawn with grey cloud above, grey cloud on all sides, and also grey cloud below.

According to O G Jones, Sphinx Ridge is good for the moral fibre of the average Englishman. The clutch and clamber is good for the physique: what's good for the morale is the open-eyed acceptance of peril for no purpose whatever.

So we admire the courage and in particular the Englishness of Atkinson on Pillar Rock, or Haskett Smith soloing the Napes Needle. There seems nothing strange about folk risking (slightly) their lives to reach some local high-spot of the earth. And in the great ranges, people have accepted almost certain death for the sake of a particularly elevated high-spot. I'm thinking of Haston and Whillans, heading on up Annapurna with benightment highly likely, no sleeping bags, and the knowledge that no one had ever survived a night at such altitude. I'm also thinking about Mallory and Irvine on Everest in 1924: the evidence is that they were descending Everest in the dark; the timings are right; I strongly suspect that they went for the summit knowing that benightment and death would be the likely result. (Shortly before, Norton and Howard Somervell had taken the opposite decision: Somervell, at any rate, reckoned that he could get to the top but not back down: and decided on down.)

We do this, of course, for the inherent nobility of the Sphinx route to Gable's summit. But what about the people who have died seeking the low-spot of the Lake District—and a garden stocked with gnomes? Divers placed underwater elves 45m down in Wast Water, England's deepest lake; and other divers have died seeking the garden of deepest gnomes. Police divers have uplifted the ugly little chaps: but a new gnomery has (it was reported in early 2005) been placed in even deeper water, out of reach of the National Elf (Removal) Service.

Is there any difference at all between Mallory losing his life for the summit of Everest, scramblers embracing the small but real risks of the Sphinx, and divers dying for a garden gnome?

ROUTE 14 The ascent of Napes Needle

Total ascent:	20m (60 feet)
Descent:	Same
Difficulty:	Hard Severe
First climbed:	W P Haskett Smith (solo) 1884

There must be something in this rope business, or people wouldn't carry them about. If I fell, I could only fall thirty feet. It was absurd to suppose that I should then break in half... no, I should simply dangle for a little, assure Ken's anxious head that all the blood he saw everywhere was only where I had hit myself on the way down, and then climb gaily up the rope to safety. Oh, well...

It was delightful to sit on top of the Needle and dangle our legs, and think 'We've done it'. About once every ten years it comes back to me that, in addition to all the things I can't do and haven't done, I have climbed the Napes Needle.

A A Milne, climbing in 1901,
from *It's Too Late Now*.

Anyone intending to climb Napes Needle will probably already own the climbing guide from the Fell

and Rock Climbing Club (*Gable and Pillar,* 1991, by Dave Kirby and Jim Loxham). They may, or may not, want more detail of the emotional momentum of the piece; or they may be interested in my timid but tricky variant above the Shoulder.

Walkers or scramblers viewing from the Dress Circle can use the following paragraphs by way of programme notes.

From the Dress Circle, or in the standard photo taken from there, you see the main features of the climb quite clearly. From the base to the Shoulder, the rock is split by the Wasdale Crack, directly facing you. This is the easiest way to the Shoulder. However there are alternatives which, while slightly harder than the Wasdale Crack, are still considerably easier than the final moves above the Shoulder. Starting from the foot of the Wasdale Crack and heading across right to the skyline edge is a route called the Arête (first climbed 1894): its pleasant open climbing on small but good holds is psychologically a better warm-up for the moves above. If your climbing style is ballerina rather than brute, you may also find it easier than the crack.

On the opposite side, the Wasdale Crack emerging on the back face of the Needle forms the Lingmell

*The Napes Needle, photographed by the Abraham brothers.
Wasdale Crack is immediately above the lowest figure.*

Crack (O G Jones, 1891). It's possible to pass between the two cracks through the pinnacle's stony heart; while, for those of a historic bent (and in this particular case, bent is the appropriate word), a route starting to the right of the Arête and then crossing it is credited to one E A Crowley in 1893. This is indeed Aleister Crowley, known as the Great Beast. Besides being the wickedest man alive at the time, Crowley was a promising climber and mountaineer. He climbed on K2 in 1902, where he threatened other expedition members with a revolver. Three years later he led an expedition to Kangchenjunga, reaching 6,200m. When several porters died in an avalanche, Crowley remained in his tent, writing: 'This is the sort of accident for which I have no sympathy whatever.' He was criticised by the Alpine Club for his attitude, quarrelled, and turned from Alpinism to the evil arts. I remember nothing of his route, so it's been erased from my brain either by the emanations of Evil or else, more likely, by the greater Beastliness of the part of the pinnacle above the Shoulder.

Standing on the Shoulder, you are confronted with the two top blocks, the crack between them being an obvious foothold. At this point, Haskett Smith threw up stones. One of them remained up, suggesting that the top was fairly flat and that there might be a square-cut hold at its edge. He wasn't sure if the top block was going to fall off if stood on, but up he went anyway.

Seen from the Shoulder, the bottom-right corner of the top block has been knocked away, so that the horizontal crack between the two blocks here forms a tiny triangular platform. Swing confidently off the right edge of the Shoulder, and perform a technical mantelshelf move to get your feet on this little plat-form.

The one attractive aspect of this move is that the spectators at the Dress Circle can't see it. Its unat-tractive aspect is the sudden and scary drop below you as you swing off the Shoulder. I have preferred instead to climb up directly from the Shoulder, with no handholds, and no footholds either, for two steps, and (having neither handhold nor foothold) slide back down to the Shoulder. On the second attempt, two tiny crystals give brief support to the feet—there's still nothing for the hands. Put your toes into the crack between the two blocks.

The next move is to sidle to the left corner of the block. Here you are very much visible to the watchers in the Dress Circle. Just at the corner, and just within reach, is a little rounded bulge worn smooth by the bootnails of the pioneers. This hold is only one of two in Lakeland to have its own specific name. It is, for its smallness and smoothness, the 'Baby's Bottom'. Don't look around for anything else; looking around leads to thought, and thought leads to second thoughts. Curve your hand around the Baby's Bottom and step up, get your hands on the block top, and place your feet beside your hands. (And the other named hold? It's Collie's Step, carved with an ice axe out of Moss Ghyll on Scafell.)

Haskett Smith left his hanky flying, held down presumably by the stone he'd thrown earlier. The top block does not fall off: it's said that three climbers together can make it wobble. Supposing they wanted to.

The attempt to abseil off has led to deaths: there is a rather obvious absence of an anchor. On the website of Needle Sports shop (www.needlesports.com), there are complicated directions for the leader now to fix three separate belays. I have found it simpler to climb back down, and allow my companion in turn to lead the pitch, protected by me from the Shoulder. The descent of the Wasdale Crack is certainly easier than the ascent above the Shoulder. It is, however, important to avoid sliding in too deep. According to legend, trousers have been lost in the Wasdale Crack, along with somebody's glass eyeball.

When I first climbed the Needle, it was graded V Diff. Perhaps it was impossible to believe that Haskett Smith, way back in 1884, had soloed a Severe. Or perhaps the Baby's Bottom has become still smoother, though even in 1966 I noticed no conspicuous ruggedness about it. Perhaps it's just that the Wasdale team got tired of rescuing people off the top. For whatever reason, today the route is graded Hard Severe.

At the back of the Needle, next to the main face, is the Obverse Route (Siegfried Herford, 1912). While the normal route has got harder, this has retained its original Hard Severe grade, so that in the graded list of the 1991 Guide the two routes stand next to each other. Accordingly, if you can't get up the top pitch from the Shoulder, in theory you could switch into Obverse Route by heading to the right, with hands in the crack below the top block, to go up the corner facing Needle Ridge. In 1928, a party including H M Kelly made a direct route from the Gap, graded Very Severe.

So things stood until 1999, when, for the first

time in 71 years, Wasdale was abuzz with the news of a new way up the Needle. In the narrow strip of rock between Herford's route and Kelly's, Stephen Reid had put up Sick Heart River (22m, E3 5c).

The Needle remains a popular and emblematic climb, despite what is by modern standards its low grade. For more than a century it has been the logo of the Fell and Rock Climbing Club; more recently, that of the Wasdale Mountain Rescue Team. A Keswick outdoor shop is named after it. A 2m-high picture of it adorns the wall of Westmorland Services on the M6. It is, quite simply, the symbol of Lakeland climbing. Confronted with its shafted, knob-topped shape, do you need me in Chapter 2 to say specifically what sort of symbol? And to get up on top of that, yes, does require some balls.

14 Rock climbing

On Easter Day 1934, exactly 50 years after his first ascent, the 83-year old W P Haskett Smith ceremonially returned to the top of Napes Needle.
'Tell us a story!' shouted the watchers from the Dress Circle alongside.
'There is no other story,' Haskett Smith replied. 'This is the top storey.'

Recorded by Harry Griffin,
Inside the Real Lakeland, 1961

A pleasant, inoffensive sport like golf, with which I dallied many years ago, is not to be spoken of in the same breath. Golf demands a considerable co-ordination of the hand (or arms) with the eye and is carried on in agreeable surroundings. But rock climbing demands the co-ordination of every muscle and every sense—apart, perhaps, from smell—and is carried on among the most beautiful and dramatic scenery in the world.

Harry Griffin,
Inside the Real Lakeland, 1961

What's the point of the Napes Needle?

Rock climbing started on Great Gable with Haskett Smith's solo ascent of the Napes Needle. Development of the sport since then has been three-stranded, like the climbing rope itself: the climbers, their gear, and the crags they climb on.

That three-stranded image comes from the Fell and Rock Climbing Club Journal of 1936. Today, climbing rope is multi-stranded, all wrapped in a woven nylon sheath: and many climbers use two of them. Meanwhile, the sport, obligingly following the Fell and Rock Club's simile, has itself become more complex and even tangled. The climbers strive to make things harder and more dangerous, even as the equipment inventors strive to make things easier and safer but above all more expensive.

And even the crags change and develop. It's not just that bits drop off—although a pinnacle graded V Diff in the 1931 Guidebook has fallen out of Eagle's Nest Gully. It's more that climbers see crags in new places, or see old crags differently. The areas of blank rock between the climbs become the climbs. In this process, Great Gable has gone into terminal fashion decline. Indeed it has done so, like the flared-trouser look of the 1970s, on two separate occasions. And yet by 2004, in what could be called the 'Routes Between the Routes Between the Routes' era, the hardest climb in England was on Great Gable's Tophet Wall.

Over 1,000 years ago, Lancelot was jousting with fourteen knights in succession and breaking their lances. In the fifth century St Simeon Stylites spent at least thirteen years on top of a pillar in the Arabian desert. Blondin walked across Niagara on a wire with the Prince of Wales sitting on his shoulders. It's always been fun to watch something uncomfortable, dangerous, and absolutely pointless. It becomes sport when you make up rules to make it harder, and then practise to make it easier; at which point it gets too easy, so you make up more rules. Rock climbing is about persuading yourself to believe things that aren't, actually, the case. It's an adventure in ethics.

The 'easy routes' era: to 1880
The implausible idea of it arrived originally from the Alps. First, you have to develop a need to reach a local high point of the Earth's crust. There's something so special about a summit: you just know it. Then it's straightforward—you simply find, and take, the easiest available way. But if that high point is Little Mell Fell, or even Skiddaw, the easy way up is much too

easy. So you carefully choose your high point so as to make the easy way up as hard as possible. Even so, in Lakeland this only really works with Pillar Rock (Moderate, 1826, Atkinson).

Pillar Rock was climbed solo, and the safety situation was simple. If you fell off, you died. In 1884 Haskett Smith climbed Scafell Pinnacle (Mod) without 'ropes or other illegitimate means'. In the same year, he founded the modern (or at least the twentieth-century) sport of rock climbing by similarly soloing the Napes Needle, 'feeling as small as a mouse climbing a milestone'. A cheerful looking chap with a sad, sad walrus moustache, Haskett Smith accompanied his climbs with appropriate epigrams from Homer and the ancient Greeks.

The gully and chimney era: 1880–1900
Of Lakeland summits, only Pillar Rock, Helm Crag, and various pinnacles offered summits that were at all hard to get to. So they thought up a different reason for doing it. Up until 1900, the point of it was to practise for the Alps. And in pursuit of that plan ice axes were carried, even in midsummer.

The easiest way up through a crag is by the gullies. In winter, these may even be snow-filled and

W P Haskett Smith

vaguely Alpine. In summer, however, one soon real-
ises that gullies are where rock masses have cracked
and moved past each other. The gully bed is an example of fault-line shattering, and accordingly loose and
rather nasty.

Lakeland rock is so good that even the gullies are
only half-bad or even pretty good; giving us Jack's

Rake (Easy, date unknown, by Jack who may even have been a sheep) or Deep Ghyll on Scafell, climbed in 1882 and featuring the foothold carved by Professor Collie's alpenstock.

Smaller and steeper than the gullies, and altogether more climbable, are the chimneys. Oblique Chimney (70ft, Diff) on Gable Crag was climbed by a large party in 1892. The second ascent, led by O G Jones, took place the following January. The walls of the chimney were iced, and the pair climbed through swirling snow to emerge into darkness and blizzard. This climb carries a winter grade of IV, but this was exceeded when Engineer's Chimney alongside (first ascended by the Scots, Glover and Ling, 1899) was re-climbed 'with a considerable amount of ice in it' at Easter 1910. This is Grade V. Winter climbing, developed as a separate sport in Scotland, took until the 1950s to reach the standard of these mock-Alpine ascents.

For these climbs the party was roped, climbing together or with primitive belays. All too often the rope's best effect was that if one fell off, so did everybody else. Thus it was in 1903 on Scafell Pinnacle, when a rope of four, on a windy day, all fell and died together.

The ridge and rib era: 1890–1905

The typical Alpine route is a ridge rather than a couloir. Needle Ridge (Diff, with the V Diff first pitch added in 1911) was climbed by Haskett Smith two years before his inaugural ascent of the Napes Needle. Indeed, to reach the Needle in that momentous September of 1884 he first descended Needle Ridge.

Needle Ridge was climbed in the Age of Gullies; but in 1892 the true Ridge Period was inaugurated by a fine climb of the exposed Eagle's Nest Ridge, which is the next one to the left of the Napes Needle. Graded Severe, it was climbed by a party including Cecil Slingsby but led by G A Solly, on a cold April day: the most skilful Lake District climb so far, and also probably the scariest. 'Exposure' is the climbers' term for emptiness underfoot. This not generally found in gullies, but the tiny Eagle's Nest ledge has lots of it. Two days later West Chimney (Diff) scurried back into the shadows of the Chimney Period, but Arrowhead Ridge Ordinary (V Diff, Slingsby again) confirmed the age of climbing in the open air.

The Abraham brothers of Keswick, who photographed all these people in action, were fine climbers themselves, especially when not encumbered with 20lb of glass-plate camera. They introduced techniques of fixed belays, such that the non-climbing members of the rope attached themselves to a rock-spike, or to a pebble inserted in a crack. This led to an improved level of safety whereby if the leader fell the strain came on the belay; and while the hemp rope would often then break, the remaining members of the party would survive, uninjured apart from rope burns.

Most crags aren't as rich in ridges as the Great Napes. By the end of the century, all of the ridge-lines

Needle Ridge, the easiest of the Napes ridges

had been climbed. So that Owen Glynne Jones could write, in the Climbers' Club Journal of 1898:

> *Ten years ago, the Cumberland fells were large enough for all. But with this terribly rapid growth of the 'tooth-and-nail' industry, we find that additional space is required ... So far as the English school is concerned, there is no more room, and not many problems remaining unsolved.*

'Tooth-and-nail school'? The nails were in their boots, but these early climbers also occasionally used bite-holds in turf.

Owen Glynne Jones

'Jones was a Londoner of Welsh descent. He was certainly eccentric, but perhaps it would be an exaggeration to say that he was mad.' So writes Adrian Bailey, in *Lakeland Rock: Classic Climbs with Chris Bonington*.

In a shop window in the Strand, Jones was gobsmacked by the classic Abraham Brothers picture of climbers on Napes Needle. 'They must be mad,' said the passing Londoners. 'Yes, yes,' agreed Jones, 'but how did they get there?' He soon found out by experiment, only to get stuck on the top and have to be rescued by nearby climbers.

However, he quickly developed into the strongest climber of his time. It was Jones who devised the 'Moderate—Difficult—Severe' grading system still in use today (although now modified with ten extra E-grades on the top). His party piece was the Billiard Table Traverse at the Wasdale Head Inn, a complete circuit with hands on the table edge and feet high on the wall behind. As the wall was lath and plaster, the feet once went through into the next room. Climbing as much in winter as in summer, he dipped his fingers in boiling carpenters' glue against frostbite.

It's particularly odd that a Jones 'it's all over' quote should close off the Ridge Era, above. For his ascent of Scafell Pinnacle from Lord's Rake (in socks, 10th April 1898) is considered the first of the Slab and Wall era, leaving the natural ridges and gullies for the bare areas between. On a wet day in 1893 he abandoned the Billiard Room to climb Kern Knotts Chimney (190ft, Diff). This was England's first outcrop problem: short and steep, with considerable climbing interest but quite irrelevant to the question of getting up Great Gable. A few years later, he climbed the much harder Kern Knotts Crack (70ft, Severe) in a style almost 1980s: first on a top rope, then as leader, and finally solo.

As well as extremely strong arms, the 'Only Genuine' Jones had a BA in Physics and a wicked sense of humour. This is shown not only in his style of rock climbing, but in the Welsh phrasebook he supplied to fellow climbers heading for Ogwen Cottage. In the menu section, one item was marked as a particular treat. The climbers' eventual order caused considerable surprise: their request had been for a boiled baby.

His climbing was advanced, but his early death, in 1899, was in nineteenth-century style. In a roped and guided party on the west arête of the Dent Blanche in Switzerland, the leader (not Jones) was overcoming an awkward passage using his second and his ice axe as footholds; inadequate belays meant that when the leader fell, so did everybody else. One man in fact survived, but only because the rope broke.

The slab and wall era: 1903–1960

Between the world wars, the Great Napes was the busiest climbing ground in England: a quarter of all Lakeland's climbs were on Gable. The Slab and Wall ethos anticipated by O G Jones on Kern Knotts was developed on the sides of the Napes Ridges, and more particularly on the fine steep wall at the right-hand end of the Great Napes overlooking Great Hell Gate.

Tophet Bastion: that's not a Norse name, surely? In fact it's Hebrew, and a concise but classy way of saying 'stands above the gate of Hell'. The actual Tophet (or more commonly Gehenna) is a suburb of Jerusalem where once were practised the idolatrous rituals of Baal, but in biblical times was a dump where the black smoke of burning garbage rose by day and dirty flames by night. Climbers of 1919 would also recall Rudyard Kipling's Himalayan adventure story *Kim*, with its chapter-head lines addressing:

Ye who tread the narrow way
By Tophet-flare to Judgement Day.

The development of Tophet Bastion started in 1919 with the same-named climb, made by H M Kelly and graded V Diff. Things got harder. Guidebook writers (Kelly edited the 1937 Fell and Rock Guide) like to make work for themselves, and he followed up with Tophet Wall (245ft, Hard Severe) in 1923; G S Bower put up the VS Innominate Crack on Kern Knotts (60ft, 1921) alongside O G Jones' classic lines. To name a place as Innominate, that is Nameless, was a favourite joke of the pedantic and professorial climbers between the wars, seen also at Innominate Tarn. The col on the other side of Gable that the Ordnance Survey marks 'Beck Head' is called 'Nameless' by the Trevelyan Huntsmen of Chapter 10.

The habit of climbing down as well as up derives from the Alps ethos: on the Zinal Rothorn, it's sometimes more convenient than setting up an abseil. But it persisted as part of Lakeland climbing right through the Slab and Wall era. In the 1940s, my father would follow an ascent by descending something two grades easier: up Eagle's Nest Direct or Tophet Wall (Severe), then down Needle Ridge or Eagle's Nest West Chimney (Diff). Alternatively, he'd continue upwards by a route on Westmorland Crag.

While the old-style Napes ridges are mountaineering routes in the general direction of Gable summit, a new rationale was needed for the Wall Era. This was the Natural Line—any way of going up rock that was appreciably easier than whatever was on either side.

This new, harder rationale was helped by a new sort of shoe. Lightweight tennis shoes, known as rubbers, meant an end to the scraping of soft iron and the click of hard steel against the rocks. It also ended the rather rapid scratching away of Lakeland's footholds. Nevertheless, there were protests against the use of '… a rubber shoe / With a thin sole, to grip on smooth or rough' in a poem by A W Andrews in the Climbers' Club Journal of 1941. Today's specialised rock shoes are expensive, and rather uncomfortable; but they are also indecent, verging even on immoral. Presumably Andrews would have disapproved equally of waterproof breathable gear worn by today's walkers. If the good Lord hadn't intended us to get wet, why did he send Great Gable more rainwater than anywhere else in England?

The use of belays at the tops of pitches, introduced by the Abraham brothers in the Ridge Era, meant that the second up a climb was adequately protected. Running belays were now being made by passing the climbing rope behind a natural or inserted chockstone or pebble; from the 1920s running belays also used slings over spikes, with a karabiner linked into the climbing rope. This made things slightly safer for the leader as well. The leading climber of his age, Colin Kirkus, wrote in *Let's Go Climbing!* (a book aimed at the children of 1941): 'Climbing is not a dangerous sport if you follow the rules … If you do make a mistake and fall off, you have quite a good chance of being held by your second man if the rope is being managed correctly.'

Even so, on the hardest climbs, the necessary spikes for runners were usually not available; and a leader falling through a distance of twice the run-out would often break the hemp rope. Fred Botterill gave us that lovely climb Abbey Buttress (V Diff, 1909) on the Eagle's Nest Ridge. More famously, he climbed Botterill's Slab on Scafell (1903), in nailed boots, ice axe between the teeth. In 1909, climbing just to the right of Abbey Buttress on Eagle's Nest Ridge, his leader (Rennison) fell from 70ft up the pitch, having placed no runners. The rope broke and Rennison died; Botterill never climbed again.

Despite (or conceivably because of) this danger to the leader, the natural lines on the rock walls of Lakeland were all drawn up in this era of rubber shoes and hempen rope. So much so that, by 1937, Astley Cooper could write in the Fell and Rock's Gable Guide: 'On the Great Napes, the energy of Kelly and others has left little for further explorers.'

Needless to say, just three years later, Lakeland quarryman Jim Birkett started to fill in the gaps on Tophet Bastion with Tophet Grooves (1940, Hard VS). If you've climbed all over it up-and-down, then climb it sideways. A 'girdle traverse', from one side to the other across a crag, has the advantage that climbing horizontally is usually more difficult and less protected for the second man. The Tophet Girdle (1944, VS 4c) was achieved by another celebrated climber, Yorkshireman Arthur Dolphin. Yorkshire gritstone, with its cracks, rounded holds and short, technical, routes, trained climbers of this era up new sorts of moves such as the abrasive hand-jam.

Astley Cooper in 1937 had been wrong. But now, with not just the natural lines exploited but also the harder lines between, and the girdle traverse crossing it all the other way, the rubber-erasing poet A W Andrews quoted above could write (in the Climbers' Club Journal of 1954): 'A new ascent is of course always exhilarating, but with the present guide-books very little is left on British crags.'

The roadside crags era: 1940s–1970s
Andrews' remark naturally heralded another huge upsurge in the sport of rock climbing. That upsurge, though, was in a downhill direction. Only a few eccentrics such as myself walked to the summit after a climb—pursuing some antique ideal of the 'all-round mountaineer', or perhaps using up the afternoon so as not to be obliged to get scared on a second rock route. Climbing was not only separated from any

idea of going up a mountain, but actually opposed to it. High crags had nasty weather, and a walk of more than ten minutes from the car was an oppression.

While the roadside crags of Borrowdale were being stripped of their ferns and moss and entered minutely into the new guidebooks, up on the Great Napes I was finding the game altogether safer (some would say, tamer) than ever before.

Nylon ropes, introduced after the war, were not only lighter and easier to handle: their strength and, more importantly, their stretch meant that a leader who fell would almost always survive. In the 1960s came nuts: small metal chockstones threaded on wire or cord. Insert one in a crack for an instant running belay. The first ones were actual nuts, lifted from the workplace by Midlands climbers such as Joe Brown the plumber. The extra runners now meant that a leader who fell would usually not even be seriously injured. Then in the 1970s came the Whillans harness: a leader who fell would be quite comfortable, and climb back up to fall again.

As the game got safer, it was also getting easier. Specialised shoes—the first made by Pierre Alain and called PAs—combined the friction of rubbers with the stiffness of a mountain boot. At the same time, the players got better at it. From the 1970s, Reinhold Messner was showing that the training methods of an Olympic runner would also help you get up Everest. In Lakeland, Pete Livesey was climbing harder by giving up smoking and going to the gym.

An extra grade of Extremely Severe (ES) was introduced to go above Very Severe; then came Exceptionally Severe (XS); then the adjectives ran out and were replaced by the E-grades E1, E2 and upwards for ever.

The style of climbing called 'Artificial', using hammers, pitons, drills, bolts and little ladders, was justified on the grounds that everything climbable by normal means had now (as in 1898, as in 1937, as in 1954), been climbed. Artificial climbing never caught on in Lakeland; and Livesey delivered it a terminal blow on Goat Crag, Borrowdale. He climbed an artificial route called Footless Crow without artificial aids, so he didn't just make the previous climbers look small, he made them look naughty as well. The thing overhangs all the way up, and is graded E5.

What counted as a climb, now, was anything that could be defined in a guidebook without overlapping on other climbs alongside. The interesting ethical questions were of how much protection and preparation were appropriate. Should some element of risk remain?

The climbing wall era: 1970s–present
Through the rest of the century things carried on getting safer, with mechanical camming devices called Friends replacing nuts. Things carried on getting easier, with chalk for the fingertips and sticky resins for the bootsoles. And things carried on getting harder, with climbers not just keeping fit and laying off the alcohol, but training specifically for the rocks on artificial indoor walls.

The 1990s also saw 'sport climbing', with running belays placed in advance by abseiling down the rockface. Is sport climbing truly sporting? Pete Whillance put up Incantations (E6) on Gable's Tophet Wall in 1984 for the television series *Classic Climbs with Chris Bonington*. Interviewed for the accompanying book by Adrian Bailey, he spoke out against the practice of abseiling down a new route, cleaning it with wire brushes, and placing running belays in advance. 'A lot of the climbs I put up are very, very serious. Serious to the extent that you may kill yourself if you fall off.' (In the 1950s, such life-threatening climbs were described simply as 'bold'. And in the days of hemp rope and no runners, such climbs were the only climbs there were.)

But such purity of ethics could mean not getting up it at all, leaving it for anyone less scrupulous coming along tomorrow. And in the event, Whillance abseiled down it in advance with a wire brush, and pre-placed a peg runner for the 20m overhanging wall of Pitch 2.

'To discover an unclimbed route up Gable,' wrote Adrian Bailey admiringly, 'is rather like trying to create a fresh advertising approach to detergents or breakfast cereals.' Accordingly, in millennial year 2000, Lakeland's hardest route, at the newly-invented grade E10 7a, was Breathless, again on Great Gable's Tophet Wall. 'The climbing is merely E8 to the good hold but then increases steadily in difficulty, with the final move being the hardest,' reported its climber, John Dunne. 'Don't fall off!'

'Not the hardest,' suggested Dave Birkett, who repeated it in 2004. 'In fact, not too bad at all.'

When, eventually, every point of upright rock is within hand's reach of a route to the left and another route to the right, there really will be no more new to do. That point is still, top climbers assure me, some distance away. And new quarries are still being carved and then closed down. Meanwhile, the old ethics never really die, they just get downgraded. Today's scramblers are still in the gully era, going up the gills unroped in ordinary walking boots and not considering themselves particularly heroic but simply finding fun. And many rock climbers are happily exploring the era 1890–1940, scarcely bothered by the fact that modern protection methods have taken away the life-threatening edge. While in the 21st century, followers of Haskett Smith, but on rather harder climbs, are once again climbing unroped and solo.

And whatever your ethos, you'll find your ideal route somewhere on Great Gable.

ROUTE 15 Little Hell Gate

Distance: 3km (2 miles) from Wasdale
Head; 5km (3 miles) from
Seathwaite in Borrowdale
Total ascent: 800m (2,600ft)
Terrain: Scree.

How good? Atmospheric and interesting, but tough.

From Wasdale follow Gavel Neese (Route 2) and turn
right along the Screes Path. From Borrowdale, take
Route 11A to Sty Head and the Screes Path (Route
12), to the scree crossing of Little Hell Gate.

Head up the screes, which are less nasty than those
of Great Hell Gate. I made my way up the left edge,
with handholds and some grass walking on the flank-
ing White Napes. Sphinx Rock is on the right-hand
gully wall. As the scree narrows between rock walls,
it bends right, so that the outflow below is no longer
visible. A rock tower appears to block the scree top;
when you reach its foot, fork right, still on scree.
Level with the top of the rock tower, turn right, off
the scree, to a grassy ridge, a component of the upper
Sphinx Ridge. A path forms on the ridge flank above
the scree, or take the ridge itself very pleasantly. Either

way, you reach the grassy neck between the top of the Great Napes and the main mountain.

Cross the neck leftwards to the main mountain, and take a path leftwards below the foot of Westmorland Crag. The path turns back right, up scree mostly. As the slope eases, contour to the right, along the top of Westmorland Crag, past a boulder supported on a stone, to Westmorland Cairn.

Head straight uphill to Gable's summit rock knoll.

Looking down Little Hell Gate

15 Little Hell Gate
Intimations of a life of going up Gable

The approach is pleasant ... a green and verdant carpet unfolds along the rising ridge, and ahead there is a promise of great interest to come in the fretted outline of the Napes; the sandwiches are not yet eaten, and the birds are singing. But at 1,500ft ... the grass ends and the scree begins ... ahead is a shifting torrent of stones up which palsied limbs must be forced. Only Moses Finger, 100 yards up, gives secure anchorage for clutching hands until a cairn is reached fifty swear-words higher, where a more solid track (the South Traverse) rises to the right ... to the obvious scree-shoot of Little Hell Gate.

Here ... the horrors recommence in even more virulent form.

A Wainwright, *The Western Fells*, 1966

Behold the Child among his new-born blisses,
A six years darling of a pygmy size! ...
Whither is fled the visionary gleam?
Where is it now, the glory and the dream?

Wordsworth, 'Ode: Intimations of Immortality'

At the age of eight I was taken up Great Gable. My memory tells me that the route was, basically, starting at Wasdale Head and then straight up to the summit. But I wasn't the man with the map that day, and I've never given that particular map-memory any real belief. For would an eight-year old ever get taken up the route where Wainwright says: 'Only when the top of the gully [Little Hell Gate] is gained is anguish dissipated by smiles'?

More reliably, I remember that the grown-up who did have the map that day walked 20 metres ahead, stopped occasionally to let my little legs catch up, and then, three seconds before I arrived, walked on. I remembered small peppermint confections called Pan Drops, left on pathside boulders for me to find as I reached them one or two or three minutes later.

The summit I do not recall at all. Only the peppermints, and the boulders, and that presumably illusory memory of where the route was. And then, about 45 years later, I had occasion to visit Little Hell Gate. And I suffered an Intimation.

Wordsworth, seven years old and lost and coming across a moonlit gibbet near Penrith, experienced an Intimation of Immortality. 'Shades of the Prison House begin to close / Upon the growing Boy.' The shades in my case being the high rock walls of Little Hell Gate. I recognised the romantic name of the place; and I recognised the place itself. The rock of the White Napes under one hand, the shifting stones, now several inches further away, and less sharply seen out of eyeballs 45 years older. The screes above, converging and bending round a corner. The tower of Westmorland Crag closing off the top.

And on the right-hand skyline, looking in with a silent sneer, the Sphinx. 'What do you think you're doing?' it was riddling silently as always. The answer then was easy. Going up hills was what people in my family did. Accordingly, it was self-evidently a sensible thing to do. Today, and even with a further generation of Turnbulls persuaded up Gable, that answer is less convincing.

The route by Little Hell Gate gives interesting views of the map-carrier's favourite rock climbs on the Great Napes and its Needle. The top of Little Hell Gate—supposing eight-year-old legs should make it that far—has the finest view in England, with the Napes ridges plunging in pinnacles immediately underneath and Wasdale 'trailing clouds of glory' westwards towards the sea. I have to say that I don't remember that view, particularly. What I remember is the stones. And not ever quite catching up. And, of course, the Pan Drops. Peppermint is, we are told today, addictive...

At about the same time, I was being taken out in small dinghies. I already knew, from an intense study of the works of Arthur Ransome, that dinghy sailing was intensely exciting. But after a couple of days of being told to 'ready about' and being expected to do that, I never sailed again. But the intensely depressing stones of Little Hell Gate had somehow got into my soul.

'Heaven lies about us in our infancy,' as Wordsworth explains. Evidently this is the case, even, in Little Hell Gate on Great Gable.

ROUTE 16 Great Hell Gate

Distance: 3½km (2½ miles) from
Wasdale Head; 5km
(3 miles) from Seathwaite
in Borrowdale

Total ascent: 800 metres (2,600ft)

Terrain: Scree.

How good? As the name suggests, this is a stimulating place, full of force and atmosphere, not to mention nastiness.

> *Where Great Gable*
> *Plunges down in carmine scree*
> *Through rock pillars to Wastwater*
> *And the heartbeat of the sea.*
> *Once I'd only to remember*
> *That sheer scree-shoot and the wind*
> *Making silences more silent*
> *To become both deaf and blind*
> *To the beast roar of a city*
> *Where I earned my daily bread.*
>
>   Thomas Blackburn, 'Hell's Gate'

From Sty Head, follow the Screes Path (Route 12)

across two sets of scree and up broken ground to a point below the bottom-right corner of the Great Napes. Here the Screes Path heads off left, across a narrow scree run, soon to pass below Napes Needle.

Turn up the left edge of this narrow scree to reach the bottom right corner of the Great Napes. Contour round to the right, to find yourself below the very steep side-wall called Tophet Bastion. You can scramble the rocky grass, along the foot of the Bastion, but must eventually move to the right, to the shifting screes of Great Hell Gate.

Grovel in the gravel, making some sort of upward progress while passing to the right of the Great Hell Gate Pillar. (According to the climbers' guide, a 'simple scramble' leads from behind to its top—it looks harder than that to me.) After quite a bit more shifty slither you reach a band of grass, and rise rapidly to the neck above the Napes Ridges. Above, on the main mountain, is the small Westmorland Crag. Pass to the left of it on a rough zigzag path, and contour back right, along the crag's top, to reach Westmorland Cairn.

Empty the pebbles from your shoes, wipe the blood from your hands, and enjoy that famous view. Then head straight up to Gable summit.

16 Hell's Gate and stairways to Heaven

'What religion have you?' Ali asked. 'Christian?'
'I haven't got any special religion this morning.
My God is the God of walkers. If you walk hard
enough, you probably don't need any other God.'
Bruce Chatwin, *In Patagonia*

The Moses who Trod up from Wasdale Head and across the Ennerdale face of Great Gable was Moses Rigg, whisky-smuggler and stealer of plumbago. But the original Moses trod up Mount Sinai, and at the top he met God.

The prophet Elijah met Him on a different hill. First there came a rushing mighty whirlwind, making it hard even to crawl to the cairn, inducing adrenalin surges and the thrill of mountain adventure. But the whirlwind was not God.

Then there came an earthquake, and various spectacular lighting effects described as fire in Heaven. But the earthquake and the fire were not God.

Finally there came a still, small voice out of the heart of the whirlwind. And the still, small voice was God.

Great Gable from Dore Head on Yewbarrow

Outdoor instructor Colin Mortlock has written a whole book (*Beyond Adventure,* Cicerone 2001) about his discovery of 'an ultimate truth or essence that links everything in Nature into an infinite unity.' Cicerone hasn't been a publisher of devotional literature, but the discoveries in Mortlock's book are religious ones. 'Everything in Nature is alive in its own way ... the rocks and the clouds, the rivers and the stars.' His experience in the mountains has also revealed that 'those closest of friends, who had died in my early years, in an essential sense were and always would be still around.'

The moment in Great Hell Gate that convinces you that God exists in every pebble and that there is, indeed, life after death: this is, to the one who experiences it, totally convincing. Much more convincing than any normal everyday evidence or argument. To anyone else, so long as we haven't yet met the ghost of Siegfried Herford from Chapter 9, it's not convincing at all.

Mortlock writes almost apologetically: mystical religion is not part of the normal stock-in-trade of outdoor instructors. But he has not been the first to find God in the great outdoors. The seventeenth-century poet Thomas Traherne, whose climbing ground was Calver Hill, north-west of Hereford, wrote in *Centuries of Meditation*:

I was entertained like an Angel with the works of God in their splendour and glory. All time was an eternity, and a perpetual Sabbath. The corn was orient and immortal wheat, which never should be reaped, nor was ever sown. The dust and stones of the street were as precious as gold. The green trees when I saw them first ravished and transported

me, their sweetness and unusual beauty made my
heart to leap, and almost mad with ecstasy, they
were such strange and wonderful things.

For Wordsworth, as for Mortlock, these transcendent moments were found particularly on the high fells. As direct input from the Infinite to the ordinary walker, they can't be communicated in cold type: but they can be expressed, as it were in-between the words, in verse.

A motion and a spirit, that impels
All thinking things, all objects of all thought
And rolls through all things.

Sitting beside a waterfall or on a mountain top was recognised in medieval China as a valid way of attaining enlightenment. Everythingness is not dissimilar from nothingness; what cannot be expressed in words is best spoken of with extreme simplicity. So, the experience of Heaven in Great Hell Gate finds itself in the koan of Dogen:

In me is no mind;
when I hear rain from the roof,
the raindrop is me.

And on Great Gable, between two footfalls on the scree of Great Hell Gate, one becomes a pebble and the entire Universe. Maybe it is merely an aesthetic reaction to the Moderately Big. Maybe it's an instinctive recognition of good leaping-out spots and escape routes. Maybe it's an exercise-induced flood of endorphin chemicals to the brain. But from time to time—at Westmorland Cairn at dawn, running down Green Gable in the cloud, stepping on the top block of Napes Needle—comes an encounter with the Beyond. And what we get on Great Gable feels like the reason for being here at all.

Such feelings cannot be communicated or explained: not even by Wordsworth. There is, after all, no reason for being here. The moment of stillness at Westmorland Cairn has no meaning, outside that particular moment, at that particular time and place. There is, almost certainly, no God. But there is Great Gable.

Rock climbing
Gable and Pillar, by Dave Kirby and Jim Loxham, 1991, Fell and Rock Climbing Club

Winter Climbs in the Lake District, Bennett, Birkett and Davison, new edition in preparation, Cicerone

Climbing/scrambling
Scrambles & Easy Climbs in the Lake District, by Jon Sparks and Judith Brown, 2003, Grey Stone

Scrambling
Scrambles in the Lake District: North, by Brian Evans, 2005, Cicerone

Walking
A Pictorial Guide to the Lakeland Fells: Book Seven The Western Fells by A Wainwright, 1966, Frances Lincoln, reprinted 2003

The Lakeland Fells, edited by June Parker and Tim Pickles, 1996, Fell and Rock Climbing Club

Geologising
  Lakeland Rocky Rambles by Bryan Lynas, 1994
  Sigma Press

Borrowdale Fell Race is organised by Borrowdale Fell-runners Club (*website:* www.borrowdalefellrunners.co.uk). The Trevelyan Hunt is by invitation only (so organise your own version). Occasional trips to the Seatoller blacklead mines are organised by the Lakeland Mining Museum, Otley Road, Keswick CA12 5LE (www.keswickminingmuseum.co.uk).

Wasdale general information and Great Gable webcam are at www.wasdaleweb.co.uk

Index

179

If you have enjoyed this book and
would like information on other
Millrace titles, please get in touch
or have a look at our website:

www.millracebooks.co.uk

Millrace
2a Leafield Road
Disley, Cheshire SK12 2JF

tel: + 44 (0)1663 765080
email: viv@millracebooks.co.uk